Blockchain and Supply Chain Logistics

"Essential reading for anyone who wants to understand why blockchain technology is critical to next generation supply chain infrastructure. We are just at the beginning of this exciting journey. This book provides real world use cases in food, healthcare, transportation, retail, manufacturing, even reverse logistics, while explaining the challenges and potential pitfalls. It is a window into our future."

—Sandra Ro, *CEO Global Blockchain Business Council, USA*

"Since people began seriously commercializing blockchain-related technologies about five years ago, Supply Chains have been one of the fastest moving applications. This is one of the first pieces of published research that shares how Blockchain Supply Chains are working, what are the benefits, implementation challenges and further research needs.

This book has been written for students, but will be of interest for anyone interested in technological innovation, government and industry. The book is especially timely during the Coronavirus Pandemic as we have seen in stark reality the fragility and lack of transparency in international supply chains."

—Dr. Jane Thomason, *CEO of Fintech Worldwide*

"A timely book on blockchain dealing with various aspects of the supply chain. An easy to read book with many applications and illustrations.

I highly recommend it."

—Samuel Fosso Wamba, *Professor, TBS Business School, Toulouse, France*

Nachiappan Subramanian · Atanu Chaudhuri ·
Yaşanur Kayıkcı

Blockchain and Supply Chain Logistics

Evolutionary Case Studies

palgrave
macmillan

Nachiappan Subramanian
Brighton, UK

Atanu Chaudhuri
Durham, UK

Yaşanur Kayıkcı
Istanbul, Turkey

ISBN 978-3-030-47530-7 ISBN 978-3-030-47531-4 (eBook)
https://doi.org/10.1007/978-3-030-47531-4

This Palgrave Pivot imprint is published by the registered company Springer Nature Switzerland AG
The registered company address is: Gewerbestrasse 11, 6330 Cham, Switzerland

Preface

This book serves as a text for students to learn the nascent emerging topic where it is rare to find materials for supply chain operations and its applications. The book contains both concept and its applications and use cases in vital sectors. The book demystifies the grey area of block chain technology and its application in several sectors. The book starts with a review of evolution of information technology in logistics till blockchain with the description of basic terminologies.

The book covers major industrial sectors such as food, healthcare, manufacturing, transportation and retail. Majority of contents are from our research projects carried out globally over the last two years. Some of the unique features of the book are empirical studies to demonstrate the application of blockchain technology in different sectors with the offering of research framework and open research questions for scholars to pursue their further studies in these topics. Simple narration of concept and detailed insights from primary research information within each chapter will enable readers to get further clarity and better understanding of blockchain technology applications. Use case narrative will provoke the readers to demystify the myths in application of concepts and the advancements made in the sector till date. We are confident the book will trigger both the academic community and practice to advance contributions to deal with existing technological challenges and relevant applications. We made sure to blend well the contents to meet the expectations of both academic and practice community.

We are very thankful to Royal Academy of Engineering who awarded a Distinguished Visiting Fellowship Mission project to the authors to study the food loss and waste in Turkish perishable food supply chain. During and after completion of the project the authors learnt the need for a book on technology interventions in logistics and supply chain. Specifically on the topic blockchain technology applications when we organized several workshops in Turkey with support of academia, professional consortium and respective country administrative authorities. This is our first joint text publication and we hope to write on specific sectors based on readers encouragement and support. We are highly indebted to our university leadership team for their great appreciation and recognition. The support of Economic and Social Research Council (ESRC) is greatly acknowledged, thanks to Jacqueline O'Reilly and the Digital Futures at Work Research Centre.

Finally, our sincere gratitude goes to Jessica Harrison, Editor for Scholarly Business, Palgrave Macmillan for giving us this opportunity to write an authored book on this topic and Ashwini Elango from production team for her patience and continuous support to bring this book out.

Brighton, UK — Nachiappan Subramanian
Durham, UK — Atanu Chaudhuri
Istanbul, Turkey — Yaşanur Kayıkcı

Contents

About the Authors

Nachiappan Subramanian (Nachi) is the Professor of Operations and Logistics Management & Supply Chains at the University of Sussex UK. Nachi has 21 years of teaching experience in the UK, China, Australia and India and two years as a consultant. He is Fellow of Chartered Institute of Logistics and Transport (CILT) UK and a Senior Fellow of Higher Education Academy, UK. Nachi has published 97 peer reviewed refereed research papers in the leading operations management journals. His research areas are technology interventions in supply chain, sustainable supply chains (environmental and social/humanitarian issues), risk and resilience, and performance measurement.

Dr. Atanu Chaudhuri is an Associate Professor of Operations and Technology Management at Durham University Business School, UK and an Adjunct Associate Professor of Operations and Supply Chain Management at Aalborg University, Denmark. Dr. Atanu has more than 8 years of industrial experience having worked in automotive industry, consulting and research- all in India and more than 9 years of academic experience in India, Denmark and UK. He was awarded as the Teacher of the Year in 2017 by Aalborg University's Study Board of Industry and Global Business Development.

He has published in leading journal of Operations and Supply Chain Management and has more than 35 journal articles to his credit. His research focuses on supply chain implications of additive manufacturing, applications of digital technologies in supply chains, supply chain risk management and resilience. He is the Senior Associate Editor of *International Journal of Logistics Management*.

He is also the Digital Supply Chain working group leader of the leading AM network—Mobility Goes Additive. Dr. Atanu has spoken on additive manufacturing applications in spare parts at industrial conferences in Sweden and Denmark.

Dr. Yaşanur Kayıkcı is Consultant and Assistant Professor at Department of Industrial Engineering, Turkish-German University in Istanbul, Turkey. She was the Head of Department of Industrial Engineering between 2015–2019. She received her B.Sc. in Industrial Engineering from Yildiz Technical University. She completed her M.Sc. in Industrial Engineering from Graz University of Technology and her M.A. in Management Organizations at Istanbul University. She obtained her Ph.D. in Information Business and Logistics Management from Vienna University of Economics and Business. Through her long professional as well as research career, she has worked with well-known international companies as management consultant and project manager and with research institutions as lecturer and university associate in the field of logistics and supply chain management for more than 24 years. She received numerous fellowships and funds from EU, FFG, FWF, DAAD, TUBITAK, Newton Funds, RAEng for her projects. She has been as a visiting researcher/professor at several universities including TU Dortmund, TU Chemnitz, TU Berlin, Vaal University of Technology, Penn State University, University of Trieste for capacity building, curriculum development and teaching activities. She has published articles in journals including *Journal of Business Logistics*, *Expert Systems with Applications*, *Business Strategy and the Environment*, *Journal of Enterprise Information Management*, *Resources, Conservation & Recycling* and among others. She conducts research on new technologies and innovations (Industry 4.0,

Logistics 4.0, IoT, blockchain, big data, on-demand tech), information systems in logistics and SCM, collaborative business models, decision support systems and modelling, sustainability, circular economy and urban mobility.

List of Figures

CHAPTER 1

Information System Evolution and Blockchain

Abstract Blockchain is the digital ledger used by the extended network to record activities along with the time stamp. The purpose of this chapter is to trace the information technology evolution and blockchain's impact on supply chain. Overall, the chapter will enhance the understanding on potential research issues in supply chain, the status quo of blockchain applications and its limitations with the prescription of suitable theories and methods. Finally, the chapter concludes with open research questions. The major outcome of this chapter is to; (i) Understand the research opportunities in blockchain from supply chain perspective. (ii) Compare and contrast blockchain applications and limitations. (iii) List the major research questions in blockchain enabled digital supply chain.

Keywords Information technology · Evolution · End-to-end supply chain · Blockchain applications · Research directions

1.1 Introduction

Information technology revolutionised logistics and supply chain and its contribution is substantial. Treiblmaier (2018) traced the information technology support in various stages starting from 1960. In late 60s and 70s progressive computation has been extensively used in logistics planning for randomized storage and to optimize inventory in managing

N. Subramanian et al., *Blockchain and Supply Chain Logistics*,
https://doi.org/10.1007/978-3-030-47531-4_1

warehouse and subsequently IT has been used to develop simplified route planning for trucks. In 1980 when personal computers emerged it has been used to support planning activities in logistics. Later in 1990, networking of computers and enterprise resource planning packages transformed linkages between companies and automated various process such as facilities to organize virtual meetings, tracking orders and order-deliver processing. As we all know in 2000 internet's dominance substantially reconfigured supply chains on upstream and downstream members' coordination activities. Typical activities are internet supported purchasing, computer aided relationship management and emergence of electronic market places. Later in 2010, IT becomes inseparable in logistics and supply chain ranging from product development, customer relationship management, computer aided manufacturing and radio frequency identification for tracking. Now in the digital era supply chain are gearing towards linking of enterprise resource planning across organizations in the tag of blockchains and embedding transparency in transactions of the end-to-end supply chain. From the above, we have seen the contribution of information technology to physical distribution, however, blockchain is completely reshaping the supply chain to encompass all the information and financial transactional activities.

According to Provenance (2015), blockchain enhances supply chain transparency by allowing every partner to access to information concerning the activities within the supply chain, such as providing customers with the ability to evaluate the products before making a decision. More specifically, blockchain is a distributed database that is based on cryptographic proof instead of trust, which allows two consenting parties to conduct a direct transaction between themselves instead of using an intermediary (Swan 2015; Pilkington 2015; Korpela et al. 2017). Thus, blockchain is a decentralized ledger recording all transaction information within a peer-to-peer (P2P) network to verify and authenticate (Arias and Shin 2013; Swan 2015). In blockchain, records and data are secure, traceable and auditable (Kouhizadeh and Sarkis 2018). The first Blockchain was conceptualized by Nakamoto, the founder of a digital currency Bitcoin (Nakamoto 2008). Blockchain alone does not utilize the advantages of the technology. Implementing emerging technologies with blockchain not only solves the visibility and traceability challenges in supply chain, but also facilitates connectivity and increases transparency. Blockchain technology can clearly be used in business to business (B2B) transactions, Internet of Things (IoT) and machine-to-machine (M2M) integrations (Korpela et al. 2017). The world is getting more connected; therefore, organisations are placing billions of devices, sensors and actuators in their products and infrastructures. Therefore, IoT and blockchain technology integration is emerging, in the near future, blockchain systems will work solely with data automatically generated from physical IoT devices in the whole supply chain (Banker 2018; Rejeb et al. 2019). Moreover, combining blockchain's distributed ledger framework with these applications and other emerging technologies such as smart mobile devices, artificial intelligence (AI), augmented reality/virtual reality, edge cloud computing, RFID and 5G are especially important in autonomous decision making. Notably, blockchain, IoT, AI and 5G complement each other and could provide shared benefits in form of more reliable data, more secure transactions and auditable capabilities (Gartner 2019; Pavithran et al. 2020). This distributed ledger technology can have profound implications for supply chain sustainability (Kouhizadeh and Sarkis 2018). The fundamental of blockchain are explained in Chapter 2.

Overall, blockchain implications in supply chain is referred as an under-researched topic (Treiblmaier (2018). There is a possibility of applying blockchain technology in the logistics industry by allowing all participants to access information about what went into producing and ordering regarding a known product (Robinson 2016). At the same time, allowing every touchpoint in the supply chain to be tracked, recorded, which increases the supply chain information transparency (Brown 2016; Korpela et al. 2017).

1.2 Motivation

Recent studies are replete with finding and identifying improvements to the current challenges and limitations of blockchain (Swan 2015) as well as the security and privacy issues in blockchain (Aitzhan and Svetinovic 2016), but efforts related to the application of blockchain in different industries and its benefits and challenges are markedly insufficient and meagre. To overcome this a systematic literature review of block chain application has been carried out by Casino et al. (2019). A detailed mindmap abstraction of the different types of blockchain applications has been developed by Casino et al. (2019) which includes data management, financial, integrity verification, governance, internet of things, health, education, privacy and security and various industry. Interestingly, the study exposes the lacunae of research in ensuring security and privacy in application of blockchain in supply chains. In addition, interoperability and adoption has been an issue in several applications including citizenship and education services such as query, verification, integration and adoption. Use of blockchain as auditable trails for automated decision making in supply chain are expected soon in supply chains. Many past studies are concerned with the key advantages of implementing blockchain in a SC environment, focus on the benefits it can offer to improve transparency and visibility of tracking activities in business operations (Chang et al. 2019). Moreover, blockchain can be considered as a technology that can offer an adequate number of solutions for cybersecurity and protection of privacy (Kshetri 2017). Blockchain Technology (BT) is tamper-proof, immutable and hack-resistant due to its architectural characteristics. Hence, BT can play an important role in preventing security breaches, while enhancing SC connectivity (Min 2019). In addition, another crucial role of BT could be the creation of end-to-end transparency, allowing companies to gain trust and confidence within their SCs (Cole et al. 2019).

There are a few attempts to explain the potential applications of blockchain to develop resilience in supply chains. Min (2019) explained the feasibility to use blockchains to mitigate risks in intermediary intervention, cybersecurity challenges, compliance on regulations and contractual disputes to enhance supply chains resilience towards uncertainty. Similarly, Makhdoom et al. (2019) studied the practical issues in terms of security and performance of integrating IoT devices with blockchain. In terms of security, the authors investigated the issues related to trust less environment, data security, device security, key management, user security and access control. Similarly, in terms of performance requirements the authors included autonomous systems, fast transaction confirmation time, low memory requirements, low communication complexity and scalability.

Hence this book considers some of the above practical issues in different industrial supply chains and explains the challenges in addressing them.

1.3 Challenges

This section discusses issues related to generic blockchain technology, research challenges in terms of theory development and open research questions in supply chain applications.

Blockchain technology is an amazing tool for supply chain to build trust, transparency, and authenticity of transactions. However, there are several limitations in terms of data handling, data characteristics, organizational support and financial readiness. On the data handling side there are concerns in volume of transactions the system has to handle for each authentication is substantial which is referred as transaction throughput. Similarly, each transaction needs considerable time to add data to blockchain which is referred as latency. Moreover, the size of data is represented as bytes per transaction which is enormous and it requires substantial computational support and finally the immutable data characteristics is disadvantageous to some applications where it is impossible to erase data. On the organizational side support from top management team, technical expertise, financial commitment and infrastructure are the key support. Besides these there are issues with scalability of application to the extended supply chain network.

Researchers are enthusiastic to know the pathways to evolve research questions in the context of blockchain application and use of suitable methods to study the phenomenon. In the past with the advent of new technology researchers widely used innovation adaption theories such as diffusion of innovation and technology adaption theories to understand the influence of newer technological development such as RFID, ERP and 3D printing. In the innovation adaption category researchers are interested to study the key elements, innovation characteristics, stage of adoption process and adopter categories. The other aspect researchers are interested to understand are the behavioral characteristics with the support of theories such as TRA (Theory of reasoned action), TPB (theory of planned behavior), TAM (technology acceptance model) and UTAUT (unified theory of acceptance and use of technology). There is also the possibility for scholars to study the organization structures with the inclusion of blockchain technology platform in the supply chain and its influence on social system that reshapes global supply chains using structuration theory or principal agent theory. The new way of simultaneous handling of finance and information sharing could be studied using information process theory. Other than the above, there are avenues to understand the transactional aspects using institutional economics perspective. Conventionally operations management scholars are interested to theorize the management of novel supply chain using network or resource-based view theories. In terms of methods there are options either to use qualitative and quantitative methods. In particular case study research is needed to investigate the integration of hardware and software technologies.

1.4 Research Opportunities and Questions

There are several research opportunities in the supply chain to study the influence of blockchain characteristics such as immutability, transparency, programmability, decentralization, consensus and distributed trust. Few thoughts from upstream to downstream supply chain with the influence of blockchain characteristics are given below;

- How to design coordination mechanism in blockchain enabled purchasing/contracting so that all players in the chain obtain benefits for being part of the chain?
- How the dynamics of buyer relationship management will change in blockchain enabled digital supply chain?
- How to mitigate bullwhip effect in production-inventory management of the digital supply chain?
- What is the role of trust in blockchain enabled supply chain governance?
- How blockchain enabled supply chain management will facilitate supply chain risk management?
- How blockchain enabled digital supply chain will address sustainable development goals?
- What organizational enablers are needed to adopt blockchain?

There is a need to understand the potential applications, challenges and future opportunities within the supply chain by sectors such as food, healthcare, transportation, retail, manufacturing and reverse logistics.

Hence, in this book we devote one chapter each to discuss the current challenges and how effective blockchain could address those challenges.

Chapter 2, covers the basic terminologies involved in blockchain including the data format, structure of a blockchain with its capabilities. The chapter describes in detail the four types of blockchain with a specific reference to Blockchain-as-a-service and their commercial offerings.

Chapter 3, narrates the food supply chain challenges as per sustainability performance. The chapter describes blockchain application in food supply chains and outline the potential benefits. In particular, the chapter analyses the implementation barriers and suggestions to carry out further research along those directions.

Chapter 4, assess the implication of blockchain technology on the pharmaceutical supply chain. The chapter explains the status quo of recalls within the sector and how to overcome various sources of errors in pharmaceutical supply chain. The specific focus is on research issues to reduce sources of error to improve efficiency in healthcare operations and patient safety. The research model signifies the mediating role of supply chain collaboration and the moderating role of blockchain characteristics.

Chapter 5, outlines the implication of blockchain technology on transportation mobility as a sharing economy. Typically, the chapter answers how blockchain could improve operational transportation efficiency and the mobility of passengers and freight. Use cases with sharing economy concept (e.g. Mobility-as-a-Service, mobility on demand) are explained. Also, this chapter touches upon blockchain standards and regulations needed for transportation.

Chapter 6, explains scope of blockchain application in retail supply chains. The chapter describes the specific challenges such as end-to-end-visibility, anti-counterfeit, product recall, certifying suppliers and crypto payments. The chapter shares the research ideas using last mile delivery as an example and offers various research pathways.

Chapter 7, investigates the implication of blockchain technology on the supply chains of specific manufacturing sectors. Specific sectors included are automotive and aerospace processes such as sourcing, production, distribution and after-sales service with reference to spare parts delivery and availability. The chapter makes readers to critically think on combining IoT, additive manufacturing and blockchain technologies to improve supply chain performance.

Chapter 8, specifically addresses blockchain technology benefits in the reverse logistics processes. The major contribution includes a risk benefit conceptual model with the theoretical background of technology acceptance model. The chapter uses managerial insights from multiple countries to nail down the opportunities and use of blockchain technologies in the reverse logistics processes.

References

Aitzhan, N. Z., & Svetinovic, D. (2016). Security and privacy in decentralized energy trading through multi-signatures, blockchain and anonymous messaging streams. *IEEE Transactions on Dependable and Secure Computing, 15*(5), 840–852.

Arias, M. A., & Shin, Y. (2013). *There are two sides to every coin-Even to the Bitcoin, a Virtual Currency.* The Regional Economist. Available at: https://www.stlouisfed.org/~/media/Files/PDFs/publications/pub_assets/pdf/re/2013/d/Bitcoin.pdf. Accessed 21 October 2018.

Banker, S. (2018). *Will Blockchain technology revolutionize supply chain applications*. Available at: https://logisticsviewpoints.com/2016/06/20/will-blockchain-technology-revolutionize-supply-chain-applications/. Accessed 18 October 2019.

Brown, T. (2016, September 27). *Blockchain in Logistics.* LinkedIn. Available at: https://www.linkedin.com/pulse/block-chain-logistics-trevor-brown. Accessed 21 December 2018.

Casino, F., Dasaklis, T. K., & Patsakis, C. (2019). A systematic literature review of blockchain based applications: Current status, classifications and open issues. *Telematics and Informatics, 36,* 55–81.

Chang, S. E., Chen, Y. C., & Lu, M. F. (2019, March). Supply chain re-engineering using blockchain technology: A case of smart contract based tracking process. *Technological Forecasting and Social Change, 144,* 1–11.

Cole, R., Stevenson, M., & Aitken, J. (2019). Blockchain technology: Implications for operations and supply chain management. *Supply Chain Management, 24*(4), 469–483. https://doi.org/10.1108/SCM-09-2018-0309.

Gartner. (2019). *Get to know blockchain: Unlock the value for your business, now and tomorrow.* Executive Guidance, Gartner.

Korpela, K., Hallikas, J., & Dahlberg, T. (2017). *Digital supply chain transformation toward blockchain integration.* Paper presented at the Proceedings of the 50th Hawaii International Conference on System Sciences.

Kouhizadeh, M., & Sarkis, J. (2018). Blockchain practices, potentials, and perspectives in greening supply chains. *Sustainability, 10,* 3652.

Kshetri, N. (2017). Blockchain's roles in strengthening cybersecurity and protecting privacy. *Telecommunications Policy, 41*(10), 1027–1038. https://doi.org/10.1016/j.telpol.2017.09.003.

Makhdoom, I., Abolhasan, M., Abbas, H., & Ni, W. (2019). Blockchain's adoption in IoT: The challenges, and a way forward. *Journal of Network and Computer Applications, 125,* 251–279.

Min, H. (2019). Blockchain technology for enhancing supply chain resilience. *Business Horizons, 62,* 35–45.

Nakamoto, S. (2008). *Bitcoin: A peer-to-peer electronic cash system*. Available at: https://bitcoin.org/bitcoin.pdf. Accessed 1 September 2018.

Pavithran, D., Shaalan, K., Al-Karaki, J. N., & Gawanmeh, A. (2020). Towards building a blockchain framework for IoT. *Cluster Computing*. https://doi.org/10.1007/s10586-020-03059-5.

Pilkington, M. (2015). *Blockchain technology: Principles and applications*. Available at: http://inpluslab.sysu.edu.cn/files/Paper/Summary/Blockchain_Thinking__The_Brain_As_A_Decentralized_Autonomous_Corporation.pdf. Accessed 21 December 2018.

Provenance. (2015). *Blockchain: The solution for transparency in product supply chain* (White Paper). Provenance. Available at: www.provenance.org/whitepaper. Accessed 18 October 2019.

Rejeb, A., Keogh, J. G., & Treiblmaier, H. (2019). Leveraging the internet of things and blockchain technology in supply chain management. *Future Internet, 11*(7), 161.

Robinson, A. (2016). *What is blockchain technology, and what is its potential impact on the supply chain*? Available at: http://cerasis.com/2016/06/29/blockchain-technology/. Accessed 21 December 2018.

Swan, M. (2015). *Blockchain: Blueprint for a new economy*. Sebastopol, CA: O'Reilly Media Inc.

Treiblmaier, H. (2018). The impact of the blockchain on the supply chain: A-based research framework and a call for action. *Supply Chain Management: An International Journal, 23*(6), 545–559.

CHAPTER 2

Basics of Blockchain

Abstract Supply chain is one of the most important application areas where blockchain has the greatest potential to reshape the supply chain structure. Blockchain can record each sequence of transactions along the journey of product from primary raw material at source to finished goods on a shelf in a way that is accessible, unalterable, verifiable, secure, transparent and trustworthy for all parties in the network. Typical learning outcomes of the chapters are; (i) to understand the basics terminology of blockchain's distributed ledger technology; (ii) to grasp the knowledge on smart contract, shared ledger and types of blockchain systems; (iii) to gain further understanding Blockchain-as-a-Service model.

Keywords Blockchain technology · Capabilities · Types · Blockchain-as-a-Service

2.1 Introduction

One challenge in the current traditional supply chains is that business database systems being used today are deficient on multiple counts, where data transactions appears inefficient, expensive, non-transparent and vulnerable in terms of fraud and misuse. These vulnerabilities originate from reliance on centralized, trust-based, third-party systems created, such as banks and financial institutions, clearinghouses, and different

N. Subramanian et al., *Blockchain and Supply Chain Logistics*, https://doi.org/10.1007/978-3-030-47531-4_2

mediators of the entire transaction process. These centralized and trust-based database systems cause bottlenecks and slowdowns to settle transactions. Lack of transparency and susceptibility to fraud, corruption and/or other wrongdoings lead to disputes among parties in the supply chain. Dispute resolution and possibly having reverse transactions or providing insurance for transactions is expensive and can cause mostly difficulties. These risks and uncertainties may ultimately result in lost productivity, delayed deadlines, financial losses and missed business opportunities in the supply chain. As the complexity of the supply chain continues to grow, organisations have much to be benefited by addressing these challenges notably by using blockchain applications to address the major supply chain issues such as counterfeit products, visibility and traceability, and lack of efficiency (Panetta 2018).

Blockchain represents a better, more secure and viable way to collaborate and conduct business among various members of a supply chain ecosystem (IBM 2017; Deloitte 2018). As a concept, it is widely accepted in the business that blockchain could do for traceability and transparency, what the internet did for communication. Blockchain, also known as Distributed Ledger Technology (DLT), is a distributed, decentralized record-keeping system to provide transparency, data security and integrity. Blockchain involves storing digital assets (blocks) using cryptography in a database (the chain). The integrity of blockchain is based on proof-of-work with a decentralized consensus approach rather than a trust-based infrastructure. Blockchain enables multiple untrusted parties to record, validate and protect information in a permanent, immutable, tamper-proof and transparent manner on a decentralized digital ledger and on a distributed system without seeking any central authority. The network partners can access transaction flows without compromising any security issue or competitive advantage and they quickly make smart decisions. It is relatively straight forward and easy for participants to integrate into the blockchain using standard application program interfaces (APIs), protocols and open-source technology (e.g. Blockchain-as-a-Service, BaaS). As end-to-end technology, blockchain ensures traceability through integration of various online systems. Blockchain is not cryptocurrency, as it refers to the overarching technology, whereas cryptocurrency uses this technology. Transactions executed using blockchain technology or protocol s may or may not use cryptocurrency as the medium of exchange. There is no central authority to control the blockchain and ledger is distributed across many computers in the network. A blockchain ledger can record each sequence of transactions for the journey of product from raw materials at source to a finished product on a shelf in a way that is secure, transparent and trustworthy.

Blockchain technology differs from most existing information systems designs by including four key characteristics; non-localisation (decentralisation), security, auditability and smart execution (Provenance 2015). Blockchain technology can be applied to various areas from both a simple process (i.e. grow, harvest, pack, deliver) to different cases whereby potentially hundreds of steps/components are brought together to complete a finished good (i.e. a mass-produced ready meal). Blockchain technology with the integration of other new and emerging technologies provides better capability of capturing both mapping data (transparency) and operational data (traceability) throughout supply chain ecosystem.

2.2 Terminologies and Capabilities

The concept of blockchain was initially presented by Satoshi Nakamoto's white paper (Nakamoto 2008) in 2008 as an underlying technology for peer-to-peer (P2P) electronic cash system, known as Bitcoin—the first cryptocurrency. Blockchain technology is an open, decentralized, distributed digital ledger to record transactions between two parties efficiently and in verifiable and permanent way (Iansiti and Lakhani 2017). A blockchain refers to a highly scalable, decentralized P2P network with a chain of blocks. The blocks contain record of data transfer and broadcast to multiple parties in the network for verification and auditing. As a technology, blockchain puts the advantages of both P2P networks and cryptographic tools together to ensure the validity of the conducted agreement (Al-Jaroodi and Mohamed 2019).

2.2.1 Data in Blockchain

The data contained within a blockchain record comes in two forms: transaction and chain code. *Transaction*: This represents generally a simple record of movement or transformation as a block, such as "supplier A has purchased 100 units of product X from supplier B". The block can be added to the chain, which provides an indelible, immutable, incorruptible, irreversible and transparent record of transactions among parties. The first blockchain is named also as genesis blockchain, which defines the characteristics of that initial block and subsequently the rest of the blockchain.

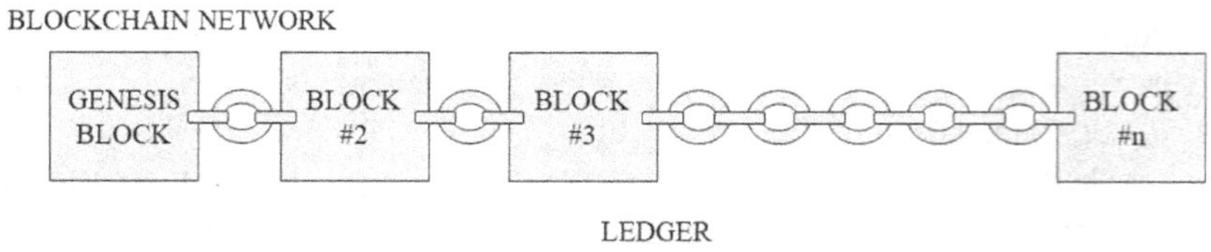

Fig. 2.1 Blockchain structure (*Source* Author)

Each transaction included in blockchain connects with the previous and next transaction. Groups of transactions are blocked together and each block with its own hash or fingerprint is added to the next, creating an irreversible chain as shown in Fig. 2.1.

Chain code: This represents the logic of so-called smart contract based on a set of rules under which parties agree to interact with each other in the blockchain and the rules cannot be broken by no one, neither the users nor the operators of the system, such as, supplier A is verified to produce 100 boxes of product X for a month and therefore cannot ship more than 100 units in a month, or product X requires ingredients Y and Z and therefore supplier A cannot produce product X, unless it has inventory of Y and Z. In practical terms, it is safe to assume that a situation such as the horsemeat scandal of 2013 would have been spotted had the supply chain recorded in this way.

2.2.2 *Capabilities of Blockchain*

Blockchain contains mainly four capabilities: shared ledger, privacy, consensus and smart contract.

(i) *Shared ledger*: Blockchain is a digitized, distributed and shared ledger among a network of stakeholders. The shared ledger generates an immutable and secure ledger of single data records. It is an "append-only" ledger of digitally signed and encrypted transactions, so every transaction logged is stored permanently and replicated across a network of participants.

(ii) *Privacy*: Blockchain provides a private, secure network for transactions among participants without mutual trust and network effects, and creates complete visibility to all parties. The privacy of the blockchain guarantees the security of individual service enquiries (confidentiality, authenticity, integrity etc.) of each transaction.

(iii) *Consensus*: As opposed to depending on a third party, such as a financial institution, credit bureau or any mediator to intervene transactions, participants in a blockchain network collectively follow a consensus protocol to agree on distributed ledger content of transactions, as well as cryptographic hashes and unique digital signatures (sort of like a username) to ensure the integrity of transactions. Entries in the ledger are synchronized to all ledgers in the network. The consensus protocol through the digitally signed transactions ensures that these shared ledgers are exact replicas and not corrupted. It reduces the risk of fraudulent transactions since record tampering would have to occur at exactly the same time across the globe.

(iv) *Smart Contract*: Smart contracts acts as the bridge which connects blockchain to the real world. Smart contracts contain business logic attached to transactions. They can automatically execute participant terms of agreements for the business that take place in the network. A smart contract is a self-executing contract embedded in computer code managed by a blockchain. The code contains a set of rules under which the parties of that smart contract agree to interact with each other. This streamlines and automates business processes that transcend organizational boundaries in a secure fashion and it forms a trust in transactions.

2.2.3 Types of Blockchain

Blockchains are not all the same. Blockchain types can be divided into four different blockchain systems: public blockchain, private blockchain, consortium blockchain and hybrid blockchain. Each blockchain type fulfils certain purposes and requirements.

(i) *Public blockchain*: known also as permissionless blockchain, mostly used blockchain type. In general, it is open, decentralized and slow blockchain system. Anyone can participate, read and write data on the blockchain network without checking authorization and has access to full data transparency. Public blockchain uses a distributed "open ledger" that allows participants to authenticate and submit data. It is highly secure and nearly impossible to corrupt, as the transaction data is validated by every participant in entire network; it is transparent, as all transactions are made public with individual anonymity. Nevertheless, because all participants on the network need to verify the transaction, it is slow and inefficient. Examples are: Bitcoin, Ethereum, Lisk, Litecoin.

(ii) *Private blockchain*: known also permissioned blockchain, refers closed and either partially or completely centralized system. Blockchain uses a distributed "private ledger" and limits participations by a central authority—owner of blockchain and mostly a single and highly trusted organisation, which has the power to control and consolidate network and give permissions who can view, read, write or validate transactions on the blockchain. This blockchain is highly efficient as verification is done by the owner of blockchain network and is private as the owner controls who what to do in the network, nevertheless, it has difficulty to align many organisations to the same blockchain. Examples are: Hyperledger Fabric, Hyperledger Sawtooth, Ripple, MultiChain.

(iii) *Consortium blockchain*: known also federated blockchain, refers partially decentralized, "semi-private" system. The blockchain network is controlled by a group of organizations, but works across different organisations. There is no consolidation of controlling power. The participants require permissions to view, read, write and verify transactions. It is efficient, as relatively lesser nodes verify transactions. Consortium blockchain is secure and helps to protect privacy. More than one organisation can act as a node and have access to exchange information and do mining. Examples included: Quorum, R3 Corda.

(iv) *Hybrid blockchain*: refers a combination of the private and public blockchain. Hybrid blockchain is controlled by a consortium of business or government entities that may both give access to the public to view or append data and may restrict access to its members (Schmahl et al. 2019). Blockchain uses both open ledger and private ledger. It uses the features of both types of blockchains that is one can have a private permission-based system as well as a public *permissionless* system. Therefore, this system maximizes the benefits of a combined public and private blockchain solution.

Companies can secure background transactions with business partners on a private ledger, while also sharing product information with customers on an open ledger. It also allows flexibility to invite more players into the blockchain. The hybrid system of blockchain is flexible so that companies can easily join a private blockchain with multiple public blockchains. A transaction in a private ledger of a hybrid blockchain is usually verified in a network, but users can also release it in the public blockchain to get verified. Examples included: Dragonchain, XinFin, Libra.

2.3 Blockchain-as-a-Service

Companies or consortia are faced typically with "make-or-buy" decision, when they want to deploy some of their services or applications on blockchain platforms. They can develop and deploy either their own in-house blockchain platforms or they can join in an existing open-source blockchain networks to run their businesses. Companies can decide on an open-source blockchain network, if their business models and governance are acceptable. If their business models are not suitable for an open-source network, they can create a new blockchain platform and they become both blockchain application providers and blockchain service providers for their own blockchain applications (Van Deventer et al. 2017). There are several open-source blockchain platform s that allows companies to create and run their own public or private blockchain projects in supply chain. This service is called as Blockchain-as-a-Service (BaaS) which has authorised infrastructure and allows consumer to use modular architecture based on the cloud-based services to develop, use and host blockchain apps, functions and smart contracts for three types of blockchain-based solutions. In nutshell, BaaS models aim at integration of standards and protocols independently by framework of specific modules in use that ease the development process. BaaS can be easily integrated in existing corporate infrastructures and business models. Several larger cloud computing providers (i.e. Microsoft, IBM, HP, Oracle, Alibaba Cloud, Jelurida) offer BaaS models. BaaS providers act as a connection between companies and enterprise blockchain platforms. The BaaS models could differ in terms of functionality, infrastructure and scalability. The companies make trade-offs and decide on an adoption of preferable BaaS model.

BaaS becomes the preferred model for providers and enterprises alike. It can significantly reduce developing costs, risks and time to market for testing and launching blockchain applications. One of the major BaaS providers, Microsoft Azure offers industry leading frameworks (i.e. Ethereum and Hyperledger Fabric) to enable companies to create private, public and consortium blockchain systems and to develop applications. Some sample of blockchain frameworks according to blockchain types are given below:

- Ethereum (https://ethereum.org/) is general-purpose, permissionless and "public blockchain" that is more suitable to describe business logic through smart contracts. All participants manage a shared open ledger without a trusted party.
- Hyperledger (https://www.hyperledger.org/) is one of the mostly used BaaS model, which provides different open-source framework s and tools such as, Fabric, Burrow, Indy, Sawtooth, Iroha and so on in order to initiate the development of blockchain and its distributed ledgers. For instance, Hyperledger Fabric is a permissioned and distributed "private blockchain" with limited number of participants (Lin and Liao 2017). It can be used in various states with specific modules and specialization for various projects like in healthcare, finance and supply chain to improve performance and reliability with the distributed ledger.
- R3 blockchain platform, named Corda (https://www.corda.net/) is consortium blockchain, launched by R3 enterprise-grade blockchain software company. Corda has a strong presence in the finance sector and provides a great deal of features such as privacy, identity, governance and many more. Corda uses private ledger, allows to have multiple parties to co-exist within one network, which are also able to interoperate within the same network system. Voltron and Marco Polo consortia use R3 Corda frameworks.
- The from Disney launched Dragonchain (https://dragonchain.com/) can be given as an example of hybrid blockchain. It is an open-source blockchain platform that has been specifically designed for enterprise and developer use. It builds private and public hybrid blockchain applications and write smart contracts in minutes with BaaS.

2.4 Key Takeaways

This chapter explain the representation of data in a block format, basic data types, specific capabilities of blockchain technology and the commercial platforms of cloud-based blockchain technology. The chapter will enable the reader to understand the terminologies when they move on the next few chapter where the application to a specific sector is discussed in detail.

References

Al-Jaroodi, J., & Mohamed, N. (2019). Blockchain in industries: A survey. *IEEE Access, 7,* 36500–36515.

Deloitte. (2018). *New tech on the block: Planning for blockchain in the retail and consumer-packaged goods industries*. Available at: https://www2.deloitte.com/content/dam/Deloitte/uk/Documents/ConsumerIndustrialProducts/deloitte-uk-blockchain-in-retail-and-cpg.pdf. Accessed 25 October 2019.

Iansiti, M., & Lakhani, K. R. (2017). The truth about blockchain. *Harvard Business Review, 95*(1), 118–127.

IBM. (2017). *Tomorrow's Value Chain: How blockchain drives visibility, trust and efficiency*. https://www.ibm.com/downloads/cas/Q2RY9RN6.

Lin, I. C., & Liao, T. C. (2017). A survey of blockchain security issues and challenges. *International Journal of Network Security, 19*(5), 653–659.

Nakamoto, S. (2008). *Bitcoin: A peer-to-peer electronic cash system* (White Paper). https://bitcoin.org/bitcoin.pdf.

Panetta, K. (2018). *Why blockchain matters to supply chain executives*. Available at: https://www.gartner.com/smarterwithgartner/why-blockchain-matters-to-supply-chain-executives/. Accessed 25 October 2019.

Provenance. (2015). *Blockchain: The solution for transparency in product supply chain* (White Paper). Provenance. Available at: www.provenance.org/whitepaper. Accessed 18 October 2019.

Schmahl, A., Mohottala, S., Burchardi, K., Egloff, C., Govers, J., Chan, T., et al. (2019). *Resolving the blockchain paradox in transportation and logistics*. BCG. Available at: https://www.bcg.com/publications/2019/resolving-blockchain-paradox-transportation-logistics.aspx. Accessed 25 October 2019.

Van Deventer, M. O., Brewster, C., & Everts, M. (2017). *Governance and business models of blockchain technologies and networks*. TNO. Available at: https://blockchain.tno.nl/. Accessed 27 October 2019.

CHAPTER 3

Blockchain Applications in Food Supply Chain

Abstract The food supply chain faces unprecedented challenges concerning human health, food security and safety, climate change, animal welfare. In addressing these challenges, ensuring transparency and traceability in the food supply chain is becoming increasingly important issue for reducing food loss and waste and ensuring food safety. In particular, digitalization and new information technologies that are rapidly developing with Industry 4.0 and their applications to the supply chain lead to significant improvements in traceability systems. One of these new technologies is blockchain. The rise of blockchain-based initiatives find use in providing traceability in bringing more transparency and efficiency to the agricultural and food supply chain. Typical outcomes of the chapter are; (i) To list the triple bottom line food supply chain challenges. (ii) To narrate the feasible tracking and tracing solutions with the support of blockchain technology.

Keywords Traceability · Validating labour conditions · Sustainability · Delivery challenges · Framework

3.1 Introduction

Food supply chains have become global and complex with multiple suppliers of raw materials and ingredients spread across the world (Roth et al. 2008). This makes it difficult to track the flow of raw materials

N. Subramanian et al., *Blockchain and Supply Chain Logistics*,
https://doi.org/10.1007/978-3-030-47531-4_3

and the products from the farm to the fork and to ensure traceability across the supply chain. Instances of food recalls have also become quite common with multiple products being recalled everyday due to quality and health concerns. This has also resulted in high profile cases like the peanut butter recall in the US, the horsemeat scandal in the UK and the baby milk powder adulteration in China. Powdered food products, spices and high value products like olive oil are particularly susceptible to adulteration. Consumers want to become more aware of the quality of the food they are consuming and will like to have the traceability information before they purchase the product. Retailers need to ensure such traceability and also track the condition of the products that is being transported.

Technologies like RFID or wireless sensor devices can be used to track the location and condition of the product respectively. Blockchain can integrate and manage each process and transaction throughout the agricultural supply chain in real time. Each transaction that is processed on the distributed ledger can carry transaction details and specific attributes for the product which can be added by members in the supply chain (Tian 2017; Tripoli and Schmidhuber 2018). Companies can input traceability information while keeping important proprietary or business-competitive information hidden. Supply chain members can identify and examine the product's movement along every step in the supply chain from the farm to the transportation and storage conditions and details as the product moves to the retailer and consumer (Tripoli and Schmidhuber 2018). Thus, Blockchain can enable retailers to share the provenance information with the customers.

3.2 Motivation and Challenges

All stakeholders involved the food supply chain (farmers, distributors, packers, processors, grocers, restaurants, traders) are driven by a need to demonstrate to their customers the superior quality of their processes and products (Smith 2008). But, this has proved to be a very difficult task because of multiple stakeholders involved in the chain and the geographical dispersion of the chain. The use cases of blockchain in food supply chain go beyond ensuring food safety. It also adds value to the current market by creating a distributed ledger in the network and balancing market price. Some of use-cases in food supply chain are given below, but these are not limited.

3.2.1 *Sharing Information for Traceability and Transparency*

Information about an end product should be as extensive, reliable and easily accessible as possible. QR code can allow sharing such information, for example, that provides access to all available information about origins of the individual components or production conditions, transportation and packaging. In food and beverage industry, such traceable, reliable information is also important for stakeholders in the production chain, so they can make sure they comply with the necessary regulations, and document that compliance. But before the data across multiple stages of the supply chain can be incorporated into the blockchain, they have to be verified by everyone involved in the network. This will provide the consumer with an uninterrupted information chain that can be examined anytime, and will guarantee that the product has been produced and transported under optimal conditions.

For example, early adopters of blockchain in the meat industry can be very successful, especially if combined with DNA codification (Sander et al. 2018). Thus, DNA samples from an animal can be used to identify its breed, and additional information such as country of origin, exposure to toxins and unregulated medication, among other key markers, can be collected. These data can be crosschecked with the blockchain record to assure the animal's authenticity and lifecycle and shared with customers (Galvez et al. 2018). Knowing the origin of meat produce has a key influence on consumers' purchasing decision process (Vukasovič 2009). Thus, a clear record of product history will improve buyer confidence that goods being purchased are from ethical sources (Saberi et al. 2019). Another example of blockchain technology adoption with using emerging technologies in food supply chain that a Chinese company, ZhongAn Online launched a blockchain-based farming program, called "GoGo Chicken" in order to provide customers to track organically farmed chickens, they have pre-purchased by using facial-recognition technology and also to monitor the health and movement of poultry through GPS tracking bracelets attached to legs. All information is recorded on blockchain ledger immutably and customers can track their movement how they grow and what they eat.

3.2.2 Validation of Labour Conditions Across the Supply Chain

Food companies and retailers have a difficult task of verifying that no unfair labour practices have been used across the supply chain. Once each worker has trusted identification represented on the blockchain, farmers or suppliers can then create and record a labour contract that specifies information such as payment terms, expected work hours or output, contract length and labor conditions. Workers can then receive payment digitally, of which the receipt is automatically recorded to the blockchain and payment confirmation is shared with organizations downstream. While blockchain is capable of recording the data, the success of this use case is predicated upon its adoption and enforcement. Similar to other labor-practice certifications, farmers and cooperatives could be incentivized to adopt this solution and in turn increase the value of their produce (Widdifield 2018).

3.2.3 Improving Quality and Avoiding Recalls

Product recalls are increasing concern for food manufacturers and retailers with lack of adherence to good manufacturing practices (GMP) being a primary reason for such recalls (Kumar and Budin 2006). Lack of capture and real-time monitoring of process data makes tracking of individual batches of production difficult. Tracking substandard products accurately and identifying further transactions of the products can help reduce the rework and recall (Saberi et al. 2019). Capturing process data using RFID or sensors and creating systems for alerts if the process parameters coupled with blockchain ensuring no tampering of data will help in real-time monitoring. This will help in improving product and process quality in production, storage and transportation and avoid costly recalls of food products.

Some challenges include tracking of fruit and vegetables sold loose that come from different farms, resistance from farmers to sharing too much information and creating complete data inputs from different nodes along a long value chain.

3.2.4 Improving Sustainability in Food Supply Chain

The outcomes of blockchain application seems to be promising in terms of sustainability gains in the form of reduced environmental impact and better assurance of human rights and fair work practices (Saberi et al.

2019). An example can be given to understand the sustainability impact of blockchain. The consumer product manufacturer Unilever built a consortium with the participation of British grocery retailer Sainsbury and packaging company Sappi in conjunction with three banking companies and pursued a year-long pilot blockchain project, called Trado model to manage transactions within tea supply chain among up to 10,000 farmers in Malawi (CISL 2019). By enabling project partners to reliably track products throughout the supply chain, the blockchain-based shared data system validated the sustainability of the tea farmers' agricultural practices easily and rewarded them appropriately. Tea farmers benefited from preferential pricing by focusing on methods designed to increase harvest without using more land. This blockchain-based project incentivized sustainable farming practices such as increased sustainable sourcing and livelihoods of smallholder farmers and made sustainable agriculture mainstream.

3.2.5 *Avoiding Food Delivery Challenges*

In a sharing economy powered by blockchain, companies have visibility in the presence of all unused logistics assets (trucks, trailers, construction equipment, warehouse capacity). Instead of waiting for customers to own and maintain fleets of logistics equipment, businesses can scale their capacity on demand. In other words, people have access to property rather than direct ownership. All participants along food supply chain can share the available unused assets on blockchain platform and utilize them.

3.3 Food Chain Use Case

French retailer Carrefour has launched blockchain information for 20 items including chicken, eggs, raw milk, oranges, pork and cheese, and will add more in the future with a focus on areas where consumers want reassurance, like baby and organic products. Customers can scan a QR barcode on a pomelo grapefruit with their phone and find out the date of harvest, location of cultivation, the owner of the plot, when it was packed, how long it took to transport to Europe and tips on how to prepare it (Thomasson 2019). Use of Blockchain to share product information with customers has resulted in faster sales of pomelo fruits and chicken for Carrefour. Sharing such information with customers is also helping Carrefour to obtain customer trust. The initiative has proved most popular so far in China—where it is already common for shoppers to scan QR codes, followed by Italy and France, with some people spending as long as 90s reading the provenance information. While Carrefour is focusing the project on its own brands, it has also worked with Nestle on giving consumers access to blockchain data for its Mousline potato puree, allowing them to see it is only made from French potatoes (Thomasson 2019).

3.4 Framework with Future Directions

There are several adoption barriers to implement blockchain technology in food chain. As per Kayikci and Subramanian (2018), nine of them are explained below with a conceptual model shown in Fig. 3.1 is developed with Technology Acceptance Model (TAM) as a theoretical reference.

Interoperability: Interoperability is the ability of different digital data to acknowledge and communicate with each another. It is a crucial for connecting business process data and humans. Process data are captured

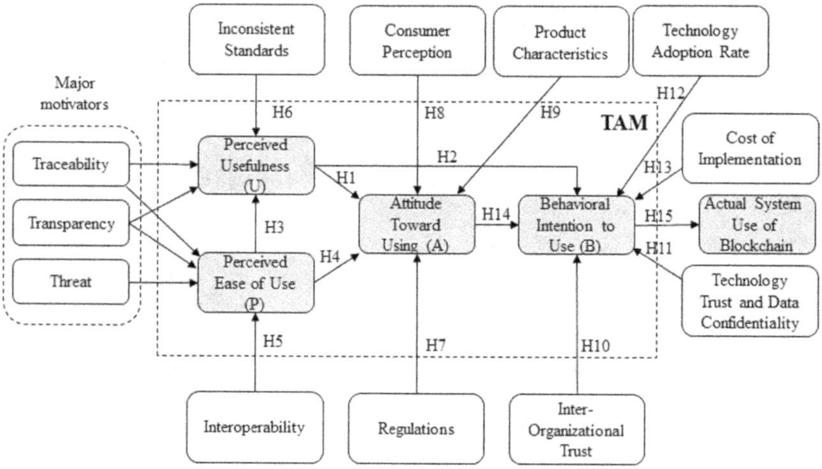

Fig. 3.1 Blockchain adoption model (*Source* Author)

from hashing, EDI, RFID, wireless sensor networks, ERP and data warehouses (Deloitte 2017; Francisco and Swanson 2018).

Inconsistent standards: Nonexistence of unique standard for blockchain technology is a serious issue for adoption (Casey and Wong 2017). There are a few initiatives to define industry standards for blockchain, one among them is the Blockchain in Transport Alliance (BiTA, https://bita.studio/) which involves thousands of companies in the transportation and logistics industry.

Regulations: There is no regulations set by industry or policy makers regarding blockchain implementation which poses a serious challenge to supply chains (Hackius and Petersen 2017).

Consumer perception: Customer preferences toward tracking food in the supply chain gains attention. If consumers are not sure about food safety and authenticity then it profoundly impacts company's bottom line (Pant et al. 2015).

Product characteristics: At the moment product characteristics such as provenance of components, material, and specifications are needed to verify by supply chain parties (Francisco and Swanson 2018). Public availability of blockchain database would reveal the characteristics to the people without any verifications.

Inter-Organizational Trust: Right now, consortium with big partners dictates the rules, which causes inter-organizational trust problems among small and medium enterprises (Hofman et al. 2017). Trust is regarded as an emergent property for honest interactions of different participants in the system (Christidis and Devetsikiotis 2016), therefore future blockchain consortium should inclusive and think about developing acceptable procedures for all partners in the supply chain.

Technology trust and data confidentiality: The data confidentiality and technology trust are important separately to verify every transaction on the distributed database before the data becomes the "undeniable truth" (Francisco and Swanson 2018).

Technology Adoption rate: As we know the acceptance and implementation depends on the higher rate of successful technology adoption of emerging technologies (Hackius and Petersen 2017).

Cost of Implementation: Cost-saving is the ultimate driver for companies to go for technology adoption (Crosby 2017). As all new technologies right now the capital cost of blockchain technology is very high because of the proof-of-work algorithm used requires significant computing power to process transactions (ESC 2017).

3.5 Key Takeaways

The chapter summarises few process and people related challenges to adopt blockchain technologies in food supply chain. The proposed research model sets out several hypotheses that would hinder various attributes of technology adoption model. These needs empirical verification from different economies.

References

Casey, M. J., & Wong, P. (2017). Global supply chains are about to get better, thanks to blockchain. *Harvard Business Review*.

Christidis, K., & Devetsikiotis, M. (2016). Blockchains and smart contracts for the Internet of Things. *IEEE Access, 4*, 2292–2303.

CISL. (2019). *Trado: New technologies to fund fairer, more transparent supply chains*. University of Cambridge Institute for Sustainability Leadership. Available at: https://www.cisl.cam.ac.uk/resources/sustainable-finance-publications/trado-new-technologies-to-fund-fairer-more-transparent-supply-chains. Accessed 27 October 2019.

Crosby, M., Pattanayak, P., Verma, S., & Kalyanaraman, V. (2017). Blockchain technology: Beyond bitcoin. *Applied Innovation Review, 2*, 6–10.

Deloitte. (2017). *Global Dairy Sector: Trends and opportunities* (White Paper). Deloitte. Available at: https://www2.deloitte.com/content/dam/Deloitte/ie/Documents/ConsumerBusiness/ie_Dairy_Industry_Trends_and_Opportunities.pdf. Accessed 20 December 2019.

ESC. (2017). *Top five enterprise blockchain challenges that must be overcome in 2018*. ESG Intelligence. Available at: https://esg-intelligence.com/blockchain-articles/2017/11/13/blockchain-challenges-2018/. Accessed 20 December 2019.

Francisco, K., & Swanson, D. (2018). The supply chain has no clothes: Technology adoption of blockchain for supply chain transparency. *Logistics, 2*(2), 1–13. Available at: www.mdpi.com/2305-6290/2/1/2/pdf. Accessed 20 December 2019.

Galvez, J. F., Mejuto, J. C., & Simal-Gandara, J. (2018). Future challenges on the use of blockchain for food traceability analysis. *TrAC Trends in Analytical Chemistry, 107*, 222–232.

Hackius, N., & Petersen, M. (2017). Blockchain in logistics and supply chain: Trick or treat? In *Proceedings of Hamburg International Conference of Logistics* (pp. 3–18). Hamburg, Germany.

Hofman, W., Spek J., & Brewster, C. (2017). *Applying blockchain technology for hyperconnected logistics*. pievent. Available at: https://www.pi.events/

IPIC2017/sites/default/files/IPIC2017-Workshop-2.2_presentations.pdf. Accessed 20 December 2019.

Kayikci, Y., & Subramanian, N. (2018). Feasibility of food loss reduction with blockchain in the merging economy context. *Proceedings of the 23rd International Symposium on Logistics (ISL 2018)* 255:261. ISBN-13 9780853583240.

Kumar, S., & Budin, E. M. (2006). Prevention and management of product recalls in the processed food industry: A case study based on an exporter's perspective. *Technovation, 26*(5–6), 739–750.

Pant, R. R., Prakash, G., & Farooquie, J. A. (2015). A framework for traceability and transparency in the dairy supply chain networks. *Procedia—Social and Behavioral Sciences, 189*, 385–394.

Roth, A. V., Tsay, A. A., Pullman, M. E., & Gray, J. V. (2008). Unraveling the food supply chain: Strategic insights from China and the 2007 recalls. *Journal of Supply Chain Management, 44*(1), 22–39.

Saberi, S., Kouhizadeh, M., Sarkis, J., & Shen, L. (2019). Blockchain technology and its relationships to sustainable supply chain management. *International Journal of Production Research, 57*(7), 2117–2135.

Sander, F., Semeijn, J., & Mahr, D. (2018). The acceptance of blockchain technology in meat traceability and transparency. *British Food Journal, 120*(9), 2066–2079.

Smith, B. G. (2008). Developing sustainable food supply chains. *Philosophical Transactions of the Royal Society B: Biological Sciences, 363*(1492), 849–861.

Thomasson, E. (2019). *Carrefour says blockchain tracking boosting sales of some products*. Available at: https://uk.reuters.com/article/us-carrefour-blockchain-idUKKCN1T42A5. Accessed 2 August 2019.

Tian, F. (2017). A supply chain traceability system for food safety based on HACCP, Blockchain & Internet of Things. In *2017 International Conference on Service Systems and Service Management* (pp. 1–6). Dalian. https://doi.org/10.1109/icsssm.2017.7996119.

Tripoli, M., & Schmidhuber, J. (2018). *Emerging opportunities for the application of blockchain in the agri-food industry*. FAO and ICTSD: Rome and Geneva. Licence: CC BY-NC-SA, 3.

Vukasovič, T. (2009). Consumer perception of poultry meat and the importance of country of origin in a purchasing making process. *World's Poultry Science Journal, 65*(1), 65–74.

Widdifield, J. (2018). *Brewing blockchain: Tracing ethically sourced coffee*. Available at: https://www.ibm.com/blogs/blockchain/2018/08/brewing-blockchain-tracing-ethically-sourced-coffee/. Accessed 2 August 2019.

CHAPTER 4

Blockchain Applications in Health Care Supply Chain

Abstract This chapter covers pharmaceutical supply chain and explains a better understanding of problems and challenges experienced in preventing product recalls in the pharmaceutical supply chain and how blockchain might alleviate recalls. More specifically, the envisaged outcomes of the chapter are; (i) A discussion highlighting the main stages and their reasons where specific product recalls related problems occur in the supply chain. (ii) The development of a product recall classification framework coupled with potential prevention strategies incorporating the deployment of emerging techniques and technologies such as blockchains. (iii) An overview of future product recall research challenges and directions for the supply chain research community.

Keywords Health care · Pharmaceutical supply chain · Product recall · Counterfeiting · Serialization

4.1 Introduction

Product recall in health care is a serious issue, which harms economic sustainability of pharmaceutical manufacturers and the health of end customers. There is a substantial increase in product recalls in pharmaceutical industry for example in the UK 63 pharmaceutical products have been recalled during 2015 (MHRA 2016). Typical recall issues are

N. Subramanian et al., *Blockchain and Supply Chain Logistics*,
https://doi.org/10.1007/978-3-030-47531-4_4

related to human involvement or oversight including tampering, labelling defects and container defects. One example in the UK context is the recall due to error in the carton of the product Primidone SERB tablets produced by Actavis, which has been printed as 250 mg instead of actual content 50 mg (Primidone 2015). Likewise, there is an exponential increase in developing countries where pharmaceutical supply chains are very complex including several companies and intermediaries before pharmaceutical products reaches the customer. Recent reports from the Chinese context suggest that there is no effective method of recalling unsold stock lying in the distribution network (Ding 2018). Given this scenario, pharmaceutical manufacturers are keen to build transparency and trust to reduce product recalls by tracing and tracking various micro level activities using advance technologies. The research in terms of implementing blockchain technology (digital ledger used to record the details of all transactions) is at an advance stage that can benefit the economic and social development of global communities. both the countries. The chapter will unleash research opportunities in pharmaceutical supply chain supporting the economic and welfare of societies.

4.2 Motivation

Pharmaceutical supply chain (PSC) comprises of drug manufacturers, logistics service providers/wholesalers, care providers and retail outlets (Ding 2018). PSC includes raw materials sourcing in the pharmaceutical manufacturing process, which can be regarded as a consolidation of Active Pharmaceutical Ingredients (APIs) and pharmaceutical excipients. Pharmaceutical products are packaged in an environmentally friendly way. After packaging, drugs are distributed by manufacturers to different third-party logistics service providers (3PLs), wholesalers and other distributors who subsequently transit drugs to hospitals, pharmacies and other retailers. In this stage, distributors have to handle reverse flows of drugs back to manufacturers due to product returns and recalls which are hazardous, so manufacturers are in a position to handle the returned drugs in a proper way. Next to distributors, the drugs will be prescribed by doctors or pharmacists to the end customers. In certain circumstances unused or unwanted drugs get accumulated in households due to mistakes in prescription, patients' death, recovery, etc. (Ding 2018). Accumulation of expired drugs can potentially contaminate the environment and it will become hazardous to human health hence it must be identified and properly disposed instead of being reused or recycled. However, the unsold or unwanted drugs, which are still conserving efficacy within their shell lives, can be redistributed, resold or donated to subsidiary market in developing countries or the people who cannot afford to buy new drugs. The PSC stages are shown in Fig. 4.1 with recalled and returned drugs. Recalls would occur at three levels in pharmaceutical supply chains such as consumer, retail and wholesale level. Food and drugs administration have classified recall into three categories such as Class I, Class II and Class III. Class I is a serious category which is dangerous to health of the patients on the other hand class III is unlikely to cause any health issues and could be having labelling or other minor errors.

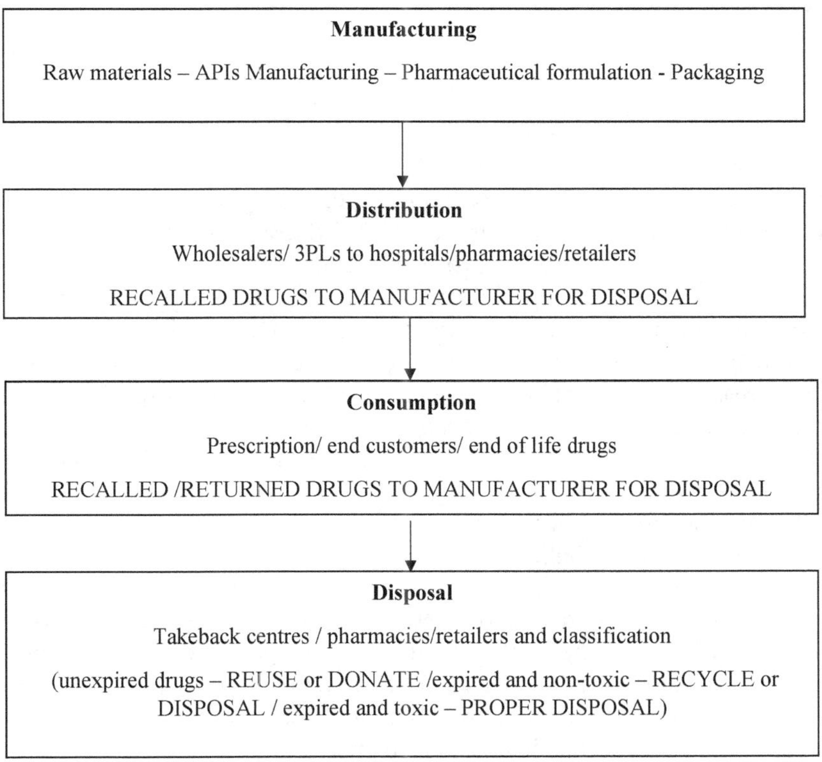

Fig. 4.1 Pharmaceutical supply chain with recall (*Source* Author)

Pharmaceutical supply chains are very vast and highly complex, for example in emerging economies pharmaceutical supply chain comprise 20,000 companies, 1000 carriers and forwarding agents, 100,000 distributors, one million retail pharmacies, 3000 locations and several thousand sales representatives. Given this scenario, it is very hard to trace and track various micro level activities for global manufacturers. Furthermore, it is a huge challenge for manufacturers to develop an excellent supply chain which achieves good coordination, reliable processes and visibility. However, recently researchers are investigating the potential of using blockchains to track and trace transactions. But so far, it is not so obvious how this technology could be used in the pharmaceutical supply chain to track and trace the various activities including the involvement of people, process parameters and time taken for each activity. It is essential to understand how blockchain could support pharma supply chains.

4.3 Challenges

PSCs are regulated by several stakeholders to ensure safety and to protect the society (Xie and Breen 2012). The objective of PSC is to deliver the right quantity of drugs with good quality, to the right place of customers at the right time with optimum cost (Jaberidoost et al. 2013). Conventional focus of PSC is to improve efficiency and profitability through cost reduction, strategy optimization, vehicle routing, best practices, etc. (Narayana et al. 2014). Although the pharmaceutical industry is still very profitable, the main goal is to guarantee its economic viability in an increasingly competing environment. Organizations without ethical and ecological conscience in supply chain management tend to lose their market share and profit (Harwood and Humby 2008). There are numerous recalls in the recent past such as cancer causing chemicals in pills and also pharmaceutical supply chain is having highest counterfeit products with $200 billion annually that has direct impact on patient safety (Shipchain 2019). The above challenges clearly depicts the need of track and trace facility to ensure safety and authenticity of the products to the final consumer. The market incubation time period for a new drug is 10–17 years and also needs a substantial investment equivalent to $2.558 billion average to release a drug (MDxBlocks 2020). A single recall due to presence of toxic materials (7%), manufacturing errors (29%) microbial contamination (29%), mislabelling (14%) and undeclared ingredients or excipients (21%) will substantially hit the bottom line of the pharmaceutical companies. In addition, with the present regulation the pharma supply chain should meet the following criteria. Allow multiple parties to update and share data, verification of information to build trust and interoperability with the regulators to ensure visibility and authenticity (PWC 2017). Involvement of many stakeholders will add complexity and longer time and to have an integrated verification system to link all the members in the pharma supply chain.

4.4 Blockchain Application Cases

This section explains how blockchain can help pharmaceutical supply chain to trace and track supply chain to reduce recall and counterfeit products.

Minimizing mislabeling: Permissioned ledger blockchain will reduce labelling inefficiency and store critical drug information by connecting all manufacturing sites regarding critical drug information for labelling in real time in a consistent and recurring format. Hence consistent information across globe and among various touch points including Food and Drug Administration will avoid drug labelling with false or misleading information (MDxBlocks 2020).

Avoiding manufacturing errors: Serialization is a mechanism of tagging the drugs from source till customer to track and trace will offer real time information to multiple stakeholder who are involved in development and to ensure the consistent specification. Hence blockchain can detect discrepancies in any stage of the pharma supply chain and helpful to improvise the supply chain standards (MDxBlocks 2020).

Track and trace and serialization to avoid recalls: FDA has created a planned implementation of a secure interoperable product tracing at a package level. To track and trace each product at a package level is highly difficult with technology available today. This is one of the challenges where Blockchain can have a significant impact in finding the solution. Blockchain offers a secure interoperable IT system that with its distributed ledger structure can have distributers, buyers and other stakeholders collaborate on the same platform. This eliminates the transfer of data between different databases that would be very difficult to achieve due to many different actors with different databases in the supply chain. Using a shared distributed ledger, it is possible for all relevant parties to securely track the product throughout the supply chain while still securing that sensitive information is not shared with any unwanted parties. Blockchain can support to trace the exact source of the batch production which went wrong with the use of serialization of tags. The tracking time has been reduced from 16 weeks to 2 seconds in a pilot project conducted by a consortium of companies such as KPMG, Merck, Walmart and IBM sponsored by US Food and Drug administration (IBM 2019). In addition to time reduction the project has several other benefits including verify a serialized drug product's validity, manage product verification requests, identify counterfeit drugs, receipt of automatic real time alerts of drug status and information about chain of custody in the event of a manufacturer generated recall (IBM 2019).

Avoiding counterfeiting: The ability to verify the parties through blockchain and their inability to change anything within the chain without full transparency in the network. There isn't a need for companies to verify every transaction of their lower tier suppliers because each at each transaction is verified for its authenticity. This also means that products are verified together with the serialization process to its authenticity. On the distribution side it makes it much more secure for the customer to know the product is an authentic product (Chaudhuri and Jochumsen 2018).

4.5 Research Framework and Future Research Directions

There are several benefits in the adoption of blockchain in pharma supply chain and there are several future research opportunities. There are multiple risks in pharmaceutical supply chains such as in transit contamination of drugs during delivery, changes in the chemical characteristics of the ingredients due to abuse of cold chain temperature monitoring and recall of drugs. Researchers can potentially analyse the moderation and mediation effects of blockchain technology and supply chain collaboration between and sources of supply chain errors and supply chain performance. Information process theory can be used as the theoretical background to understand the benefits of blockchain technology on pharma supply chain performance. Several propositions could be developed and assessed to study the relationship between the variables of constructs shown in Fig. 4.2.

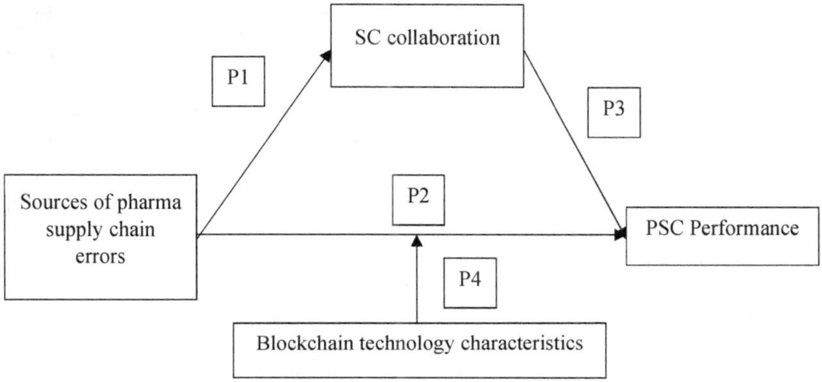

Fig. 4.2 Technology enabled pharma supply chain conceptual model (*Source* Author)

4.6 Key Takeaways

Pharmaceutical supply chain is vital for healthcare where there are several sources of errors which impacts the supply chain effectiveness and efficiency. This chapter spells out few blockchain based solutions to overcome the errors caused in labelling and manufacturing which is substantial right now. Again, there are several research opportunities to study the role of collaboration and technology intervention in pharmaceutical supply chains.

References

Chaudhuri, A., & Jochumsen, M. L. (2018). *Blockchain's impact on supply chain of a pharmaceutical company*. Presented at EUROMA Conference, Budapest.

Ding, B. (2018). Pharma Industry 4.0: Literature review and research opportunities in sustainable pharmaceutical supply chains. *Process Safety and Environmental Protection, 119*, 115–130.

Harwood, I., & Humby, S. (2008). Embedding corporate responsibility into supply: A snapshot of progress. *European Management Journal, 26*(3), 166–174.

IBM. (2019). *Protect pharmaceutical product integrity with the pharmaceutical utility network*. Available at: https://www.ibm.com/blogs/blockchain/2019/12/protect-pharmaceutical-product-integrity-with-the-pharmaceutical-utility-network/. Accessed 22 March 2020.

Jaberidoost, M., Nikfar, S., Abdollahiasl, A., & Dinarvand, R. (2013). Pharmaceutical supply chain risks: A systematic review. *DARU Journal of Pharmaceutical Sciences, 21*(1), 1.

MDxBlocks. (2020). *Blockchain for drug recall handling*. Available at: http://mdxblocks.com/blog/blockchain-for-drug-recall-handling/. Accessed 22 March 2020.

MHRA. (2016). *Medicines and healthcare products regulatory agency* (blog). Available at: https://mhrainspectorate.blog.gov.uk/2017/04/21/2016-gmp-inspection-deficiency-data-trend/. Accessed 26 February 2019.

Narayana, S. A., Pati, R. K., & Vrat, P. (2014). Managerial research on the pharmaceutical supply chain—A critical review and some insights for future directions. *Journal of Purchasing and Supply Management, 20*(1), 18–40.

Primidone. (2015). *Alerts and recalls for drugs and medical devices*. Available at: https://www.gov.uk/drug-device-alerts?alert_type=drugs&medical_specialism%5B%5D=general-surgery&medical_specialism%5B%5D=pharmacy. Accessed 26 February 2019.

PWC. (2017). *Accurate, audited and secure: How blockchain could strengthen the pharmaceutical supply chain*. Available at: https://www.pwc.co.uk/healthcare/pdf/health-blockchain-supplychain-report%20v4.pdf. Accessed 23 March 2020.

Shipchains. (2019). *Recalls and blockchain: How blockchain can aid in and ultimately prevent recalls*. Available at: https://blog.shipchain.io/blockchain-can-prevent-recalls/. Accessed 22 March 2020.

Xie, Y., & Breen, L. (2012). Greening community pharmaceutical supply chain in UK: A cross boundary approach. *Supply Chain Management: An International Journal, 17*(1), 40–53.

CHAPTER 5

Blockchain Applications and Future Opportunities in Transportation

Abstract Blockchain technology has the potential to revolutionize transportation as it can redefine and redesign entire transport management system by enabling more efficient business operations thereby increasing the profit margins. Blockchain-enabled platforms allow easier coordination of shipping/packing documents on a shared distributed ledger across transportation supply chain ecosystem, making manual data entry and physical paperwork mostly unnecessary and also reducing the counterfeiting of documents. Approvals and custom clearance can be quicker and more efficient and import/export processing times of goods can be expedited at customs checkpoints by using smart contracts. Typical learning outcomes of this topic are; (i) to understand blockchain application in transportation supply chain; (ii) to analyse the challenges and opportunities of blockchain technology in transportation industry.

Keywords Tracking · Monetisation · Delivery · Performance · Public transportation · Autonomous vehicles

5.1 Introduction

The transport industry is one of the primary beneficiaries with major players taking part in blockchain adoption. However, the industry has been struggling with security threats, logistics inefficiencies and general

N. Subramanian et al., *Blockchain and Supply Chain Logistics*,
https://doi.org/10.1007/978-3-030-47531-4_5

uncertainty, such as, empty run, underutilization, wasted fuel, unbalanced inventory. In order to cope up with these problems, transportation companies are trying to digitise logistics processes, incorporate new and emerging technologies (e.g. cloud, IoT) as well as increase connectivity and automation. Blockchain technology is one of those technologies which can transform the business and service models of transportation industry. The studies show that blockchain has been the most mass adopted technological disruption in the transportation and logistics industry (Verma 2019). Blockchain helps companies in transportation supply chain operate better and provides secure, updated and authentic data across the transportation supply chain ecosystem, since the whole network contributed to data validation. All communications and transactions along the processes in the lifecycle of transportation systems can be recorded trustworthily and immutably in the distributed ledger.

5.2 Motivation

The transportation sector is examining the application of blockchain frameworks, where more companies have been attempting on proof-of-concept testing of use cases in IoT architectures combined with blockchain to share encrypted data between parties in transportation supply chain (O'Shea 2019). Since the perception of blockchain was mostly related to the activities in cryptocurrency ecosystem due to early applications, and was not as a decentralized, distributed asset exchange technology for sharing data with partners, the lack of understanding of its potential remains a major obstacle to adoption of blockchain technology. Another hurdle is lack of the willingness of companies to participate in an open ecosystem and share the IoT generated data among ecosystem participants. Companies in transportation supply chain are working with numerous intermediaries to ship and deliver packages, where it is important to understand how data generated from one company's IoT sensors (at a port, in a warehouse or on a delivery truck) could be shared with others to refine processes and provide better customer experiences. In this regard, blockchain offers promising applications in transportation supply chains. Some of those are given below:

(i) *Data monetisation*

Blockchain helps transportation companies to generate measurable economic benefits from the large volume of data sources collected by using big data, IoT sensors and VR/AR. These benefits are revenue increase, expense savings, market share or corporate market value gains. Every organisation specializes in collecting specific types of data, which can be in transportation industry: freight volume, congestion, traffic accident and so on. These data can be bought or sold through blockchain platform. Continental and Hewlett Packard Enterprise launched a blockchain-based data monetisation platform in a strategic partnership to benefit the transportation supply chain (HPE 2019). The platform enables new digital services to improve driver safety and convenience by allowing to share the from IoT sensors collected data (providing driver-assistance services like real-time traffic warnings, locating available parking etc.) on one vehicle on the road with other connected vehicles. In the meanwhile, the platform helps car manufacturers monetize their data and differentiate their brands. Although, this platform is in its early stages, similar application can be considered to be used in truck fleet platforms.

(ii) *Reducing payment time and tracking of cargo*

According to a study (Winnesota 2019), the transport industry ties $140 billion in payments and disputes every day. Processing and administration costs due to overreliance on paper transactions have increased to as high as 20% of overall transportation costs. This can result in slower invoice transfer and delay in payment. For an average invoice, a transport company needs to wait more than 42 days before receiving payment. In addition, transport industry faces with the health of cargo along transportation supply chain due to insufficient temperature conditions. A paper-based document, Bill of Lading (BoL) is a legal contract issued by the carrier of good. Blockchain turns this document as a digital file put into the smart contracts and shares among the authorized parties in the transportation network. This can enable real-time cargo monitoring in the case of implementing smart contract s into the transportation operations. For example, the RFID tracking device at a buyer's warehouse can be directly connected to the blockchain and after receiving the cargo from the supplier, RFID can check whether the agreed quantity is delivered or not, and if there are no other conditions to be met (e.g. deliveries undergoing quality assessments and approved by the buyer), the smart contract can automatically release the payment to the supplier (Pournader et al. 2019). As the world is grappling with COVID19 virus, it is important that all players in the transportation chain are adopting good practices and ensuring that the drivers and good handlers are following WHO guidelines and sanitising the products, the different surfaces. A Blockchain based validation that appropriate practices have been followed can assure the end user that the products are safe to use.

(iii) *Efficient processing of insurance claims*

A major benefit of using blockchain technology for tracking cargo is the faster processing of insurance claims in cases where cargo has been lost or damaged. Considering that the tracking data on blockchains are trustworthy and traceable to the origin of loss, insurance companies can process the causes of the incident, the carrier involved, the type of cargo and the validity of the claims faster and easier. A recent example of such an application is the world's first marine insurance platform on blockchain called Insurwave, which leverages blockchain technology, the Microsoft Azure analytics platform using ACORD data standards (EY 2018). Insurwave can support half a million transactions and manage the risk of shipping for more than 1000 commercial vessels by connecting all stakeholders in the insuring process including third parties, clients, insurers and brokers (Pournader et al. 2019).

(iv) *Tracking fleet and vehicle performance history*

Blockchain technology provides all transportation chain parties a secure, universal and on-demand visibility over the movement of freights. The parties can track the performance of their transport units (trucks, semi-trailer trucks, trailers, maritime containers) in terms of load rate such as full-truck-load, dead-mile or less-than-truckload miles each travel within a delivery fleet. The performance and maintenance history of delivery units lead to a more reliable model of pricing and efficiency.

(v) *Common data standards*

Data standards make blockchain application smarter. Some organisations are working to create universal standards for mass adoption of blockchain technology in transportation supply chain. For this purpose,

In 2017, *Blockchain in Transport Alliance*, called BiTA (https://www.bita.studio) was formed to bring together leading technology and transportation companies to develop and embrace a common framework and universal freight standards for blockchain applications. BiTA has over 500 members from all over the world spanning the transportation and logistics, consumer goods and technology sectors. BiTA seeks to drive the industry-wide adoption of blockchain technology in logistics and transportation industry to standardize the method of tracking goods: such as recording request for proposals and transactions, fuel payment and repricing without the need for a processor, payment and settlement solutions.

(vi) *Same-day/one-hour delivery*

The retail e-commerce market has grown unprecedentedly worldwide over the years. This transforms the customers shopping experience from offline to more online shopping. According to statista,[1] in 2019, retail e-commerce sales amounted to 3.53 trillion US dollars and e-retail revenues are projected to grow to 6.54 trillion US dollars by 2023. Apparently, this is the most promising time for logistics services and start-ups to tackle the challenges in order to offer faster modes of delivery at cheaper prices. As the same-day delivery market is expected to reach 987 million[2] by 2019. However, traditional tracking technologies are not scalable to support the rising demand for same-day and one-hour delivery services. Blockchain technology and P2P model provide transport companies a scalable, immediate solution for order tracking and authentication, improve delivery performance and provide same-day/one-hour delivery for their customers. The companies such as Amazon, Shopify increase the number of online customers through offering same-day delivery options. Blockchain use-cases for same-day delivery can be seen in practice such as VOLT (https://volttech.io/).[3]

[1] https://www.statista.com/statistics/379046/worldwide-retail-e-commerce-sales/.

[2] https://www.businesswire.com/news/home/20160108005570/en/Research-Markets-Same-day-Delivery-Market-Worth-USD.

[3] https://volttech.io/same-day-delivery/.

5.3 Blockchain Application Cases in Transportation

TradeLens: Maersk and IBM joint digital shipping platform

Roughly ninety percent of world's goods are carried by the sea transport each year. The leading ocean shipping company Maersk launched with the collaboration of IBM a new blockchain solution based on Hyperledger Fabric, named TradeLens (https://www.tradelens.com/) shipping blockchain platform to manage and track the paper trail of tens of millions of shipping containers across the world by digitizing supply chain processes. The objective of TradeLens is to support information exchange and transparency across transportation supply chain and encourage innovation. The platform is expanding with the participations of other ocean carriers like Hapag-Llyod, Ocean Network Express etc. The blockchain-enabled digital shipping solution is designed to promote more efficient, secure and fast documentation workflows and deliver freight goods across international borders, also it helps to reduce fraud and errors, reduce the time spent on products in the transit and shipping, improve inventory management and finally reduce waste and cost. The recent study showed that a simple refrigerated goods shipment from Africa to Europe passed through more than 30 organisations including 200 separate interactions and communications among them (Lewis 2017) and any process interruption along those shipping processes can cause the container to be held or lost (Van Mölken 2018). Blockchain simplifies the shipping processes, records data securely and immutably and enables real-time visibility and shipment status along transportation supply chain. The blockchain platform uses a private ledger for end-to-end visibility, which is accessible only to authorized partners based on their level of permissions. Stakeholders in supply chain ecosystem can monitor the real time status of cargo along the transportation supply chain and track where cargo is in transit and they can also view all documentation including bills of lading, and customs document. No one can delete or append any record without consensus with others.

SkyCell blockchain cold chain

A Switzerland-based high-tech company, called SkyCell (http://www.skycell.ch/) has created an IoT and blockchain-enabled refrigerated air freight containers for the biopharmaceuticals cold chain reducing temperature-deviated rate down to less than 0.1%. The objective of SkyCell is to secure sensitive goods and make sure no compromised product is delivered to anyone. The company has partnerships with a number of major airlines specializing in pharmaceuticals. Since biopharmaceutical products are temperature sensitive goods, their production costs are much higher than traditional drugs, supply chain waste and loss are more costly and companies have a strong incentive to minimize it. Moreover, degradation due to temperature variation is invisible unlike food spoilage. Therefore, cold chain security and visibility are primary for biopharmaceuticals. Adoption of blockchain can solve the problems in this kind of transportation supply chain and help to track and trace the temperature of biopharmaceuticals products from manufacture to pharmacy. SkyCell records temperature data from more than 1000 temperature-controlled containers circulating through the global cold chain. The company simply put IoT sensors and data loggers on the containers and accumulate numerous data points in order to map the transportation supply chain for biopharmaceuticals products in real-time. In addition, SkyCell has started to accept cryptocurrencies for payments.

5.4 Challenges in Blockchain Adoption for Transportation

The assumption behind all potential applications is a perfect technological adaption, but logistics managers have often witnessed technological failures first hand. For example, Electronic Data Exchange (EDI) has been the standard system in the logistics industry for over 30 years, but the industry still lacks an overall EDI standard, instead, many different technologies are used (Dobrovnik et al. 2018). It cannot be assumed that multiple players in the transportation industry with age old practices will readily embrace blockchain. The benefits need to be communicated to all players and pilot projects conducted to demonstrate the benefits.

5.5 Future Opportunities

There can be potentially many opportunities for blockchain adoption in transportation. We highlight a couple of those here.

(i) *Combining Augmented Reality and Virtual Reality with blockchain*

The current web-based digital solutions for copying a photograph is trivial and it is difficult to understand whether digital photo is an original photo or just a copy of that digital photo. Blockchain addresses this issue by allowing developers to create unique digital assets that cannot be copied by anyone. In this regard, there is a need to link Augmented Reality (AR) and blockchain technology together. This solution can be also used on a blockchain platform in transportation supply chain to follow up cargo and take AR-powered photos about packing of goods, customs inspection and unpacking at destination.

(ii) *Mobility—Public transportation MaaS and blockchain*

Blockchain has the potential to align with other cutting-edge technologies in mobility and public transportation. One of these technologies is Mobility-as-a-Service (MaaS), which can integrate multiple mobility services to solve the mobility problems. For ticketing, current smart cards, e-tickets or hardcopies (traditional ticket) are used. These kinds of ticket have recently utilized either Near-Field Communication (NFC) or Barcode as state-of-the-art technologies. However, using the same technology for ticket validation between different providers is challenging since each provider has had its own scheme. MaaS can alleviate the problem by including a trip planner, e-ticket, payment method (both "pay-as-you-go" and "mobility package") and also validated ticket scheme (Nguyen et al. 2019).

MaaS can offer added value through use of a single application to provide access to mobility, with a single payment channel instead of multiple ticketing and payment operations. For its users, MaaS should be the best value proposition, by helping them meet their mobility needs and solve the inconvenient parts of individual journeys as well as the entire system of mobility services. Currently there is a pilot blockchain-based MaaS solution, called Tesseract, which has been complied by Ethereum based smart contracts. Such blockchain enabled MaaS can provide seamless mobility users to users and authenticate payments to the service providers.

(iii) *Blockchain-powered autonomous vehicles with IoT, AI and 5G*

Blockchain will be the integral part of developing autonomous vehicle. Especially, some automotive companies (e.g. Daimler) pursuing some pilots such as Mobility Open Blockchain Initiative (MOBI) for vehicle identity standards (Jenkinson 2019) to test machine-to-machine (M2M) payment s using a blockchain platform without any human interaction. Blockchain is evolving parallel with other emerging technologies in transportation: especially, Internet of Things (IoT), Artificial Intelligence (AI) and the fifth generation of wireless technology (5G) among them are the most important technologies for blockchain-powered autonomous vehicle interaction. The autonomous vehicles require the real-time processing of massive amounts of data generated from billions of devices, sensors and actuators. Combination of these technologies are especially important in autonomous decision making. Blockchain, IoT, AI and 5G complement each other and could provide shared benefits in form of more reliable data, more secure transactions and auditable capabilities. The future of blockchain require more IoT, AI and 5G application to be used in the context of autonomous vehicles. The blockchain will reserve and pay for parking, draw car to electricity to charge the car's battery (Gartner 2019). Enhanced automotive blockchain could coordinate movement of autonomous self-driving vehicles between multiple owners or within a ridesharing network.

References

Dobrovnik, M., Herold, D. M., Fürst, E., & Kummer, S. (2018). Blockchain for and in logistics: What to adopt and where to start. *Logistics, 2*(3), 18.

EY. (2018). *World's first blockchain platform for marine insurance now in commercial use*. Ernst & Young. Available at: https://www.ey.com/en_gl/news/2018/05/world-s-first-blockchain-platform-for-marine-insurance-now-in-co. Accessed 25 October 2019.

Gartner. (2019). *Get to know blockchain: Unlock the value for your business, now and tomorrow*. Executive Guidance, Gartner.

HPE. (2019). *Hewlett Packard Enterprise and Continental launch blockchain-based data monetization platform*. Available at: https://www.hpe.com/us/en/newsroom/press-release/2019/02/hewlett-packard-enterprise-and-continental-launch-blockchain-based-data-monetization-platform.html. Accessed 25 October 2019.

Jenkinson, G. (2019). *Can blockchain become an integral part of autonomous vehicles?* Available at: https://cointelegraph.com/news/can-blockchain-become-an-integral-part-of-autonomous-vehicles. Accessed 12 December 2019.

Lewis, K. (2017). *Blockchain: Four use cases transforming business*. IBM. Available at: https://www.ibm.com/blogs/internet-of-things/iot-blockchain-use-cases/. Accessed 25 October 2019.

Nguyen, T. H., Partala, J., & Pirttikangas, S. (2019). Blockchain-based mobility-as-a-service. In *2019 28th International Conference on Computer Communication and Networks (ICCCN)* (pp. 1–6). IEEE.

O'Shea, D. (2019). *Evaluating the role of IoT and blockchain in transportation*. Available at: https://www.iotworldtoday.com/2019/08/20/evaluating-the-role-of-iot-and-blockchain-in-transportation/. Accessed 25 October 2019.

Pournader, M., Shi, Y., Seuring, S., & Koh, S. L. (2019). Blockchain applications in supply chains, transport and logistics: A systematic review of the literature. *International Journal of Production Research*. https://doi.org/10.1080/00207543.2019.1650976.

Van Mölken, R. (2018). *Blockchain across Oracle: Understand the details and implications of the blockchain for Oracle developers and customers*. Birmingham: Packt Publishing.

Verma, S. (2019). *Blockchain and IoT in commercial transportation*. Available at: https://www.ibm.com/blogs/blockchain/2019/06/blockchain-and-iot-in-commercial-transportation/. Accessed 25 October 2019.

Winnesota. (2019). *How blockchain is revolutionizing the world of transportation and logistics*. https://www.winnesota.com/blockchain. Accessed 25 October 2019.

CHAPTER 6

Blockchain Applications in Retail Supply Chain

Abstract High customer expectations, product provenance and authenticity, transparency, traceability and inventory management are critical points in any retail business. The failure to provide these points can lead to customer dissatisfaction, defection and extremely inefficient processes. Retailers can stand to benefit from better provenance tools, as consumers are increasingly concerned about the origins of products they purchase, from ethical as well as value-based standpoints. The main benefit of blockchain is that retail organisations can prove what they delivered on their promises by product authenticity, tracking and tracing reliable delivery throughout the supply chain and accountability of suppliers. This chapter aim to; (i) Help retailers to understand potential application areas of blockchain in retail supply chain. (ii) Analyse the challenges and opportunities of blockchain technology in retail industry.

Keywords Product provenance · Supply chain visibility · Product authenticity · Security · Privacy · Last mile delivery · Drones

6.1 Introduction

More and more retailers keen to harness latest emerging technologies such as blockchain to help end consumers track and trace the supply chain of selling products to verify origin, location and status of goods through

N. Subramanian et al., *Blockchain and Supply Chain Logistics*,
https://doi.org/10.1007/978-3-030-47531-4_6

digitising marketing channels. Blockchain technology provides a scalable, immediate solution for order tracking and authentication. Monitoring the processes can ensure that the products get to the end consumers safely and intact. Studies have shown that the implementation of blockchain based tracking systems can increase sales and customer services in retail business. However, for the adoption of blockchain technology in retail supply chain to be successful, it must have a proven value to the customer. If retailers and supply chain partners do not benefit from blockchain, they will probably not embrace it.

Today's most blockchain projects in the retail supply chain space use private ledgers (Bidlack 2019) and they are based on either private, consortium or even hybrid blockchain. Retailers are building their own blockchains for themselves and their supply chain partners and are otherwise not available for others to use or copy. Moreover, the potential use cases mostly appear on food-related products and but also on non-food-related retail products for the areas such as supply chain and inventory oversight, accepting crypto payments, customer identity, taxation, preventing fraud and counterfeit goods, consumer demand contracts, product contracts, reducing cyber hacks, improving shared services models and so on. Particularly large retailers are establishing blockchain consortia with suppliers, logistics providers and other supply chain partners together to build their own blockchain platforms from scratch, which are not accessible out of blockchain network. Retailers also adopt those blockchain platforms with using smart tags (NFC/RFID/QR Code) to ensure visibility and traceability of the entire lifecycle management of retail products.

6.2 Motivation and Challenges

Blockchain offers significant customer-facing opportunities to enhance shopping experience in the retail supply chains that retailers should consider. Over the last year, an increasing number of retailers have started to explore the potential of blockchain to adopt in their business. For instance, Alibaba is adopting blockchain solutions for its subsidiaries in order to track its cross-border shipments effectively. Similarly, retail giant Walmart has put its fresh food products on the blockchain. There are many objectives to adopt blockchain: these include, but not limited to, product provenance, fraud prevention, management of loyalty points (i.e. customer loyalty and rewards), compliant consumer data, accepting payments with cryptocurrencies. Some of blockchain applications in retail supply chain are given as bellow:

(i) *End-to-end supply chain visibility*

Solving visibility becomes a core prerequisite for each party in retail supply chain, as this points out almost all of the other challenges that exist. The leading retailers take action to establish blockchain platforms with the collaboration of blockchain providers. IBM is one of technology company to act with retailers to develop blockchain solutions for solving supply chain visibility in the frame of IBM Food Trust Program. French supermarket giant Carrefour implemented blockchain system with the collaboration of IBM to track and trace its Quality Line products such as meat, milk, and fruit from farms to stores to improve customer trust and the profits, further the company wants to add additional hundreds non-food items to the blockchain-based traceability platform.

(ii) *Anti-Counterfeit*

Counterfeiting is a major issue in retail business. Counterfeit products have poor quality and may be contaminated. They can cause food-borne illnesses and even death. There is a need to detect contaminated and fraud products on the shelves and gather reliable data such as from which suppliers are bought and in which stores these products were sold. Blockchain can answer this challenge that encrypted ledger system allows retailers to create so called "digital passport" for goods to demonstrate movement of goods through all the way down from the origins to supply chain into the stores. US retailer company, Walmart tested blockchain pilots run on Hyperledger Fabric with the collaboration of IBM Food Trust Program and made a good progress with blockchain use-cases to detect fraud or contaminated products easily and identify the potential source of food-borne disease. Many food products like leafy green vegetables, mangoes, avocados are detected by placing the supply chain on the blockchain, which makes the retail processes more traceable, transparent and fully digital. Each party on the blockchain represents an entity that has managed the product on the way to store. The infected retail product is detected easily and faster in the retailer store and also the source of retail product is identified quickly and reliably from which farm supplies.

(iii) *Quick product recall*

The retailers have a responsibility to pull the affected products off the shelves, quickly and reliably in order to protect customers and reduce or eliminate their liability. Moreover, product recall is extremely complex, time consuming and expensive due to difficulty of tracing product back from customers, and it can cause heavy losses and even bankrupt companies. The product recall includes notifications to regulators, supply chain partners and customers, product retrieval, storage destruction, unsalable products, investigating the cause of the recall and all labour costs arising from the aforementioned activities. Typically, removal of product costs over US$10 million might take more than 10 months to identify contaminated/fraud products and remove them from store shelves. Blockchain in retail supply chain helps to identify quickly the contaminated batches and distributed stores. So that, the retailers can take a quick action for recall processes in the store before they were sold. The entire product recall can result large cost-savings in identifying problem, as instead of recalling all products, only through blockchain identified certain batches are recalled. The leading retailers such as Walmart, Carrefour and Migros pursued quick product recall from retail stores and gained great benefits with blockchain application.

(iv) *Certifying reliable suppliers*

Retailers want to work with trustworthy suppliers to delivery high quality products just-in-time, and to minimize the return and refund rate. This must be the one of major determinants of long-run successful business environment. Therefore, there is a need to set up an open, fair and transparent communication with retailers and their suppliers. Blockchain provides retailers to control the performance of their suppliers and certify their products. A larger US retailer company, Target developed a blockchain powered supply chain management solution run on Hyperledger Sawtooth, called ConsenSource (Pollock 2019), which is used to audit, certify and monitor suppliers for the company's paper manufacturing.

(v) *Crypto payments*

The crypto payment offers opportunities for retailer to benefit. The usage of digital wallets applications such as Alipay and WeChat Pay has already proven its popularity to customers outside the traditional banking system, but also cryptocurrencies can succeed in fulfilling the similar role. The retailers are currently looking for crypto payment options for their B2B and B2C customers. However, payment infrastructure for blockchain in retail business needs to improve, as it can be really difficult to set up a digital wallet right now or transfer payments to a retailer in time. Facebook launched recently a blockchain framework Libra for crypto payments based on "hybrid blockchain", where one is public blockchain for B2C customers who purchase items using digital wallets and the other is private blockchain for B2B corporate transactions.

6.3 Blockchain Application Cases in Retail Supply Chain

ConsenSource, blockchain-powered solution for supply chain management

The US based major retailer Target has started to adopt blockchain-powered solution based on Hyperledger Sawtooth, called ConsenSource for retail supply chain. The blockchain project focuses primarily on providing certification for the suppliers of the Target's paper manufacturers. The blockchain platform is communicating directly with forest managers and certification boards to determine which data should be recorded and stored in the blockchain throughout the retail supply chain. This is very helpful to solve the initial obstacles when trying to record the entire supply chain, as the greatest obstacle to implementing a distributed ledger and reaching a decentralized supply chain management system is getting multiple companies to agree on which data are stored and how the system is operated and governed. The ConsenSource platform is entirely open-source for paper supply chain solution.

Easy Trading Connect blockchain-based transaction system

Louis Dreyfus Co (www.ldc.com), a leading agricultural commodities trader in collaboration with a group of financing banks established a blockchain-based commodity platform, called Easy Trading Connect (ETC) in retail supply chain and performed the first agricultural commodity trade through the sale of soybeans cargo from US to a retailer in China covering all aspects of the operation from financing through to commercial contract execution and related logistics processes. The solution providers of this blockchain platform is Ethereum. ETC platform was designed to digitalize and standardize commodity transactions. The objective of blockchain project is to cut costs and reduce transaction and document processing times. This new technology brings a great deal of efficiency to complex commodity transactions and changes the way of buying and selling of raw materials. Even with the first application, the time spent on processing documents and data is reduced from hours to minutes.

6.4 Blockchain Application in Last Mile Delivery

The surge in demand of online retailing has forced online retailers and their suppliers to evaluate distribution network strategies. Conventionally customers can choose pick up delivery options including home delivery, store pickup or cash on delivery. All these options are the parts of logistics which is referred as "Last Mile Delivery (LMD)". Due to the fact that LMD is a key competitive for logistics companies, new technologies should be developed to enhance their delivery efficiency. Hence, an upcoming trend is 'Drones' that will enable logistics major companies to overcome the challenges of same-day or same-hour delivery, ensuring a high availability level (Troudi et al. 2018).

Drone technology is developing exponentially but there are social and civil issues involved as much than technological ones. For example, there are questions surrounding the acceptance of multiple drones in the sky over major cities. Regulatory frameworks will be needed to control the headspace over major cities and there is plenty of humor generated from the potential for mischief making, such as intervening with drones in flight or stealing the drone and delivery (Edwards and Subramanian 2014). Hence, there is a heated argument on how to track and identify all drones in the Sky or the missions of the drone program (Dronelife 2018). Various stakeholders are attempting to develop technology-based solution to address two major concerns such as privacy and security when using drone-based delivery systems. One pilot study conducted by Walmart created a repository that could log information regarding delivery operations such as time, location, resources, delivery date and made accessible to the authenticated users and other stakeholders to trace the package routes (Dronelife 2018). All these developments are in primitive stage and further study is essential to understand the viability of these technologies in practice. The question to be answered in the above context is how blockchain can improve privacy and security in drone-based delivery?

6.5 Research Framework

One among the feasible way to address last mile challenge is to collectively view the societal impact of drones and organizational readiness to implement blockchain. On the theoretical front conceptual research model shown in Fig. 6.1 is developed based on theory of planned behaviour (TPB) and technology, organizational and environmental (TOE) factors. TPB is considered as one of the most crucial models of assessing attribute-behaviour relationships that the attitude toward drone-based delivery service and its implementation intention (Ramadan et al. 2017). The factors that determine the implementation and adoption of blockchain technology for a company should be investigated by using the TOE framework. Specific factors included in societal concerns are safety concerns, security concerns, privacy concerns and customer acceptance. Factors included in blockchain applications are security and safety, traceability and transparency.

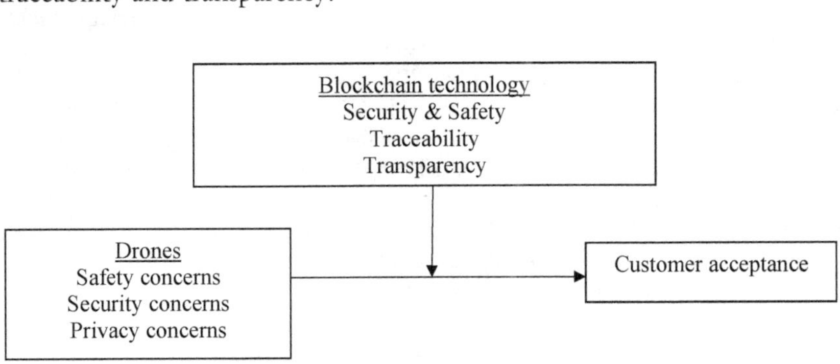

Fig. 6.1 Moderation effect of blockchain technology on the relationship between safety of drones and customer acceptance (*Source* Author)

6.6 Key Takeaways

There are numerous possibilities to study the causality between variables in blockchain adoption decision through cross cultural or longitudinal studies. Specifically, it would be interesting to study the influence of contextual variables such as industry trends, peer pressures, government intervention, extent of top management support for blockchain technology adoption decision and also the integrated effect of blockchain technology with big data analytics, cloud computing, robotics and AI tools.

References

Bidlack, B. (2019). *Blockchain is transforming the retail supply chain*. Available at: https://www.practicalecommerce.com/blockchain-is-transforming-the-retail-supply-chain. Accessed 25 October 2019.

Dronelife. (2018). *How blockchain and drones go together*. Available at: https://dronelife.com/2018/08/13/how-blockchain-and-drones-go-together/. Accessed 25 October 2019.

Edwards, D., & Subramanian, N. (2014). Delivery drones could be a reality. *China Daily*. Available at: http://www.chinadaily.com.cn/opinion/2014-06/06/content_17566985_2.htm.

Pollock, D. (2019). *Retail giant target unmasks its blockchain framework aimed at supply chain*. Available at: https://www.forbes.com/sites/darrynpollock/2019/06/10/retail-giant-target-unmasks-its-blockchain-framework-aimed-at-supply-chain/. Accessed 25 October 2019.

Ramadan, Z. B., Farah, M. F., & Mrad, M. (2017). An adapted TPB approach to consumers' acceptance of service-delivery drones. *Technology Analysis & Strategic Management, 29*(7), 817–828. https://doi.org/10.1080/09537325.2016.1242720.

Troudi, A., Addouche, S. A., Dellagi, S., & El Mhamedi, A. (2018). Sizing of the drone delivery fleet considering energy autonomy. *Sustainability, 10*(9), 1–17. https://doi.org/10.3390/su10093344.

CHAPTER 7

Blockchain Applications in Manufacturing Supply Chain

Abstract Blockchain can have potential to address critical challenges in the manufacturing supply chain if appropriate applications are chosen and multiple partners agree to collaborate for such initiatives. There needs to be a framework for choosing appropriate blockchain use cases in manufacturing. Such a framework can consider competitive priority of the firms in terms of efficiency or responsiveness and customization and whether the company differentiate itself with respect to competitors through products or services. The learning outcomes of the chapter are: (i) To highlight the potential applications of blockchain across the manufacturing supply chain. (ii) Analyse the potential challenges and opportunities for blockchain applications. (iii) Offer a framework for implementing blockchain across the manufacturing supply chain.

Keywords Validation · Avoiding fraud · Authentication · Tracking of maintenance · Supporting digital thread

7.1 Introduction

Supply chains for manufactured products have become increasingly complex with multiple tiers of suppliers, spread across the world. This makes it difficult to have visibility and ensure traceability as the products flow through the chain. To add to the complexity, such global supply

N. Subramanian et al., *Blockchain and Supply Chain Logistics*,
https://doi.org/10.1007/978-3-030-47531-4_7

chains are subjected to multiple disruptions and fraudulent practices. Counterfeit materials and products also infiltrate such complex, global supply chains.

Many manufacturers have also transformed their business models to service oriented one or on the process of doing so. This creates challenges in terms of collecting and using product usage data to develop performance based solutions for its customers. At the same time, manufacturing firms are undergoing major transformation by adopting digitalization as core of their future long-term strategy. Will manufacturers consider blockchain as part of their digitalization strategy? Blockchain can have potential to address critical challenges in the manufacturing supply chain if appropriate applications are chosen and multiple partners agree to collaborate for such initiatives. But, questions remain on how can manufacturers identify suitable use cases for blockchain applications for critical challenges they face. In this chapter, we will provide examples of suitable blockchain applications in manufacturing and provide a framework which can help manufacturers choose such applications.

7.2 Motivation

There is an increasing need to simplify supply chain processes, improve visibility and traceability and to minimize fraud and disruptions in the supply chain. Collaboration and integration of processes with supply chain partners have been attempted since the 1990s. While such approaches like Collaborative Planning Forecasting and Replenishment have provided mixed results in improving supply chain performance, most supply chains have struggled to ensure that all supply chain partners adopt synchronized processes and technological solutions. Most technological solutions require significant investments and create barriers for adoption across the supply chain. In that regard, blockchain offers promising applications in manufacturing supply chains. We highlight some of those below:

(i) *Validating supply chain transactions*

Multiple transactions take place in the supply chain related to buying and selling of goods. In the current process, validating the transactions require significant amount of time. It is also difficult to check and validity of the provenance or authentication of the good or parts sold. This is particularly challenging for re-used or recycle parts, where the buyer would like to know the usage history and record of previous transactions before buying. Blockchain makes it possible to create and share a digital ledger of transactions among various parties. The latest data, encrypted and unchangeable, can be accessible on all participants' systems. Honeywell Aerospace unit, for example, introduced an online marketplace based on blockchain that lets more than 800 international buyers and sellers trade aerospace parts in real time. GoDirect Trade was designed like a retail website. It lists items such as bolts, nuts, avionics and engine parts in different categories, along with images and the company selling the part. Airlines can also use GoDirect Trade to buy noncritical parts to fix seats or in-flight entertainment systems (Shah 2019).

(ii) *Authenticating materials procurement and supplier part approvals*

Blockchain can serve as an interoperable storage locker for necessary certifications, allowing manufacturers and suppliers to have clearer oversight into the tests being performed by the suppliers and their results. Thus, documents showing cumulative results of the part approval process and quality checks for every batch of parts supplied could be stored in a secure manner. This will play significant role in analyzing any warranty or quality failures during usage of the product and will also prove to be invaluable in cases of eventual recall of parts to trace back quality problems.

(iii) *Avoiding fraud, counterfeiting and supply chain risk*

Blockchain requires the approval of all parties in a single chain to approve data entry and changes to the ledger. As manufacturing requires continuous communication amongst supply chain partners, a single data breach could compromise the operations of each partner. Hence, the level of security provided by blockchain could prevent fraud related to tampering or misuse of data. With blockchain, it is possible for all relevant parties to securely track the product throughout the supply chain while still securing that the sensitive information is not shared with any unwanted parties. This will ensure traceability and avoid counterfeiting. For example, the largest defence contractor Lockheed Martin is working with Virginia-based GuardTime Federase blockchain technology to enhance data integrity, speed up problem discovery (Higgins 2017).

In the eventuality that a supply chain risk does occur in terms of quality lapses in the supply chain and products need to be recalled, blockchain can enable easier tracking of the faulty part across the chain. This will ensure that the root causes of the quality lapse can be quickly identified and necessary corrective action can be taken.

(iv) *Authentication of IoT devices and facilitating servitization*

Manufacturers are adopting internet of things (IoT) both for monitoring processes within their operations as well as on their products to analyze the actual operating conditions of the products. Analyzing data collected from the products' usage conditions can help in improving the product performance. Many manufacturers have started their journey towards servitization by offering performance based services. Key to offering such performance outcomes is deep understanding of usage of the products in the customers' facilities. This helps in ensuring that failure of parts in the product can be predicted and suitable actions can be taken for maintenance and for replacing the parts with spare parts. This results in proactive maintenance activities and to avoid costly downtimes. This is made possible by tracking the usage conditions of the parts by sensors and other IoT devices. This requires that equipment manufacturers are able to monitor and access the data from IoT devices attached to the equipments. For any such IoT network, the integrity of data being collected is very important. Providing a secure network by which IoT devices can be authenticated, monitored, and through which information can be securely passed along and immediately shared will be the primary use case at the intersection of blockchain tech and the IoT for manufacturing.

(v) *Tracking and optimization of maintenance activities*

Unplanned maintenance results in equipment downtime and causes serious financial implications. Ensuring safe and secure real-time data from IoT devices on equipments may help in predicting failure of parts and conduct proactive maintenance. But the actual maintenance activities also need to be tracked to continuously improve it. The blockchain provides an interoperable, single-source ledger that all parties (assuming they are participating) on a service and maintenance supply chain can consult to achieve real-time updates. Such a system is better equipped to identify and monitor maintenance progress, ultimately using that data to improve the maintenance processes.

(vi) *Supporting the creation of digital thread for additive manufacturing*

Additive manufacturing (AM) because of its digital nature ensures that parts and products are easier to share and transmit, enabling the creation of digital supply networks and supply chains. A key barrier for mass adoption of AM is the absence of a digital thread—a single, seamless strand of data that stretches from the initial design concept to the finished part (Cotteleer et al. 2016). For AM processes to scale at the industrial level, a series of complex, connected, and data-driven events are expected to occur. Thus, successfully deploying AM will require secure data and records management, referred to as digital thread for AM (Trouton et al. 2018). The blockchain for AM has the potential to serve as a backbone and security layer for the digital thread for AM, securing all the transactions that occur throughout the digital and physical life cycle for AM. It can provide a secure platform upon which designs and instructions for AM could be purchased or shared between parties for free or at a very affordable price with a measure of necessary oversight as a precursor.

(vii) *Use blockchain to develop new products and services*

Collecting product usage data from customers in a secured way and analyzing them can also help in developing new products and associated services. Blockchain may create transparency and trust among users, reduce risk of fraud so that manufacturers and their partners can use the data to develop new products (Shah 2019).

7.3 Challenges

The global supply chain operates in a complex environment that requires different stakeholders to comply with diverse laws and regulations. They include maritime laws and regulations, commercial codes etc. Since international businesses operate against the backdrop of these established old laws, customs and institutions, implementing blockchain-based solutions can be a difficult and time-consuming process (Casey and Wong 2017). Implementation of blockchain consists of bringing all the supply chain partners together, which can also prove to be difficult as any other supply chain collaboration initiative. Finally, if only a few players in the supply chain join hands to create their own blockchain, to a certain extent it will fail to take the full benefits. Moreover, such a blockchain will be more vulnerable to attack as a hacker can target a few of the participants (Kshetri 2018). Some of the challenges for adopting blockchain can be lack of a clear return on investment, immaturity of the technology, regulatory challenges, interoperability with legacy and other IT systems, security of transactions, privacy policies and lack of complementary IT systems in partner organisations (CapGemini Research Institute 2018)

7.4 Blockchain Application Cases in Manufacturing

Boeing's IoT driven blockchain to improve maintenance operations
IBM Watson IoT platform now enables devices to send data from these things to private blockchain ledgers for inclusion in shared transactions with tamper-resistant records. Blockchain's distributed replication allows business partners to verify each transaction. Through Watson IoT Platform, physical devices could be allowed to participate in blockchain transactions. Thus, IoT devices could send anything from GPS coordinates to temperature data to register or update events. One use case for IoT enabled blockchain is in parts life cycle tracking and maintenance, where it could be used to track individual part provenance from the manufacturing date all the way to disposal. During the lifecycle of an aircraft from design and build to dispoal, thousands of parts are involved. Hence, tracking each and every part along with maintaining a record of its conditions becomes a challenge. With IoT enabled blockchain, Boeing now holds complete provenance details of each component part. This information is then accessible by each manufacturer in the production process, the aircraft owners and maintainers, and government regulators. IoT-driven blockchain will work with the aircraft's digital twin to anticipate and mitigate problems before they occur. It can increase awareness of what's available from whom, and enhance the accuracy of when new parts are delivered, Thus, an aircraft's position and its in-flight performance can be tracked. When it lands, the data from IoT driven blockchain can be used to have the right parts and maintenance capabilities in place to minimize aircraft turnaround time (Gutierez 2017).

Toyota's Blockchain Initiative (Toyota Research Institute 2017)
Hundreds of billions of miles of human driving data may be needed to develop safe and reliable autonomous vehicles. Blockchains and distributed ledgers may enable pooling data from vehicle owners, fleet managers, and manufacturers to shorten the time for reaching this goal, thereby bringing forward the safety, efficiency and convenience benefits of autonomous driving technology. Toyota Research Institute (TRI) is collaborating with the LabMIT Media (MIT ML) and other industry partners to foster a digital environment where users—both businesses and consumers—may securely share driving and autonomous vehicle testing data, manage ride-share and car-share transactions and store vehicle usage information. TRI is working with several industry partners in addition to MIT ML to develop applications and proofs of concept for three areas of the new mobility ecosystem: driving/testing data sharing, car/ride share transactions and usage-based insurance.

Driving/Testing Data Sharing: Blockchain technology may allow companies and individuals to securely share and monetize their driving information and access the data contributed by others in a secure marketplace. Modern vehicles are increasingly aware of their environment through onboard sensors and are increasingly connected to the cloud, roadway infrastructure and other vehicles, all of which are generating massive amounts of valuable data. Blockchain can create an opportunity to share driving and autonomous testing data in an environment that preserves ownership of the data by the creator.

Car/Ride Share Transactions: Tools based on Blockchain have the potential to empower vehicle owners to monetize their asset by selling rides, cargo space or even the use of the vehicle itself. The blockchain can store data about the vehicle's usage and information about vehicle owners, drivers and passengers. This profile information can help validate a "smart contract" between two parties plus manage payment of services between them without need of a financial intermediary, thereby saving transaction surcharges. The system may also provide connectivity to vehicle functions for remote locking/unlocking doors and engine startup/shut off.

Usage-Based Insurance: The blockchain can also be used for vehicle owners to save money on their insurance rates. By allowing the vehicle's sensors to collect driving data and store it in a blockchain, vehicle owners may be eligible to further lower their insurance costs by giving their insurance companies increased transparency to reduce fraud plus granting them access to driving data to measure safe driving habits.

7.5 Framework with Future Directions

Blockchain should not be considered as an isolated technology but should be an integral part of the digitalization strategy of manufacturing firms. Thus, implementation of blockchain should align with the strategic priorities of the firms. We provide a framework, as shown in Fig. 7.1, which can help manufacturing companies choose the specific use cases for blockchain implementation. The framework considers two dimensions—competitive priority of the firm in terms of efficiency or responsiveness and whether differentiation is through product or service.

If a company's differentiation is through products and its priority is to improve efficiency across the supply chain, validating supply chain transactions, authenticating materials procurement and supplier part approvals and avoiding fraud, counterfeiting and supply chain risk can be suitable blockchain use cases which the company can focus on. If a company is an industrial products company also providing maintenance services for its customers, it may consider using blockchain for tracking and optimization of maintenance activities. If a company's business model is centred around

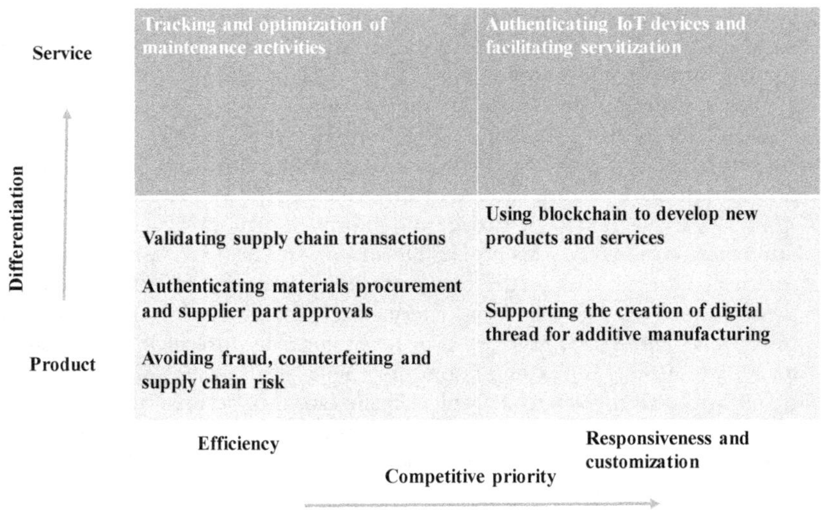

Fig. 7.1 Framework for choosing blockchain use cases in manufacturing (*Source* Author)

servitisation and its priority is to be responsive to customer needs, authentication of IoT devices to capture data from installed base and using it to facilitate servitization can be a suitable blockchain application. If the company's differentiation is through products and its priority is responsiveness and customization, it may consider additive manufacturing to develop customized parts, delivered within short lead times. But adoption of AM across the supply chain may be hampered due to lack of security of the digital thread. Thus blockchain for AM can be a suitable use case in this context. Similarly, if a company needs to collect large volumes of product usage data from customer to develop future products, it will need blockchain to securely pool data from customers and use it to develop the future products, as demonstrated by Toyota.

Before developing the business case for a Blockchain initiative, a manufacturing company needs to assess its market position, how it can influence the ecosystem, and whether it can define a standard and influence regulatory barrier change. It then needs to identify the suitable partners and develop the proof of concept with them.

7.6 Key Takeaways

Blockchain can have many potential applications in a manufacturing supply chain but a company needs to choose only a couple of the most relevant use cases which have the potential to address specific challenges in its supply chain and deliver the maximum benefits. It is also important that most of the supply chain partners related to the particular use case be involved so that they also see the benefits and agree to take part in the initiative. Care should be taken to develop a minimum viable product to demonstrate the benefits. Companies must not start blockchain projects as a management fad that others are doing unless they can justify that blockchain can address some of the most critical challenges their supply chain is experiencing.

References

CapGemini Research Institute. (2018). *Does Blockchain hold the key to a new age in Supply Chain transparency and trust?* Available at: https://www.capgemini.com/research/does-blockchain-hold-the-key-to-a-new-age-in-supply-chain-transparency-and-trust/. Accessed 1 August 2019.

Casey, M. J., & Wong, P. (2017). Global supply chains are about to get better, thanks to blockchain. *Harvard Business Review*. Available at: https://hbr.org/2017/03/global-supply-chainsare-about-to-get-better-thanks-to-blockchain.

Cotteleer, M., Trouton, S., & Dobner, E. (2016, March 3). *3D opportunity and the digital thread: Additive manufacturing ties it all together*. Deloitte University Press. Available at: https://dupress.deloitte.com/dup-us-en/focus/3d-opportunity/3d-printing-digital-thread-in-manufacturing.html.

Gutierez, C. (2017). *Boeing improves operations with blockchain and the Internet of Things*. Available at: https://www.altoros.com/blog/boeing-improves-operations-with-blockchain-and-the-internet-of-things/. Accessed 4 June 2019.

Higgins, S. (2017). *Defense Giant Lockheed Martin integrates blockchain*. Available at: https://www.coindesk.com/defense-giant-lockheed-martin-integrates-blockchain. Accessed 4 June 2019.

Kshetri, N. (2018). Blockchain's roles in meeting key supply chain management objectives. *International Journal of Information Management, 39*, 80–89.

Shah, A. (2019). *Honeywell brings blockchain to used aircraft parts market*. Available at: https://www.wsj.com/articles/honeywell-brings-blockchain-to-used-aircraft-parts-market-11559072819. Accessed 1 June 2019.

Toyota Research Institute. (2017). *Toyota Research Institute explores blockchain technology for development of new mobility ecosystem*. Available at: https://media.toyota.ca/releases/toyota-research-institute-explores-blockchain-technology-for-development-of-new-mobility-ecosystem. Accessed 4 June 2019.

Trouton, S., Vitale, M., & Killmayer, S. (2018). *3D opportunity for blockchain: Additive manufacturing links the digital thread*. Deloitte Center for Integrated Research. Available at: https://www2.deloitte.com/content/dam/insights/us/articles/3255_3D-opportunity_blockchain/DUP_3D-opportunity_blockchain.pdf.

CHAPTER 8

Blockchain Applications in Reverse Logistics

Abstract This chapter explains the potential application of blockchain in reverse logistics. Interviews are conducted with managers of well-known logistics and information technology companies in Turkey as well as Hong Kong to understand their perception about adoption of blockchain technology in reverse logistics operations. The chapter identifies perceived benefits and risks of adopting Blockchain and potentially address the existing reverse logistics challenges. Previous studies have been conducted to explore blockchain technology in different areas (e.g. banking and finance and other sector pilot studies) and its limitations. However, we are unaware of any study, which explored adoption of blockchain technology in reverse logistics operations. (i) Further guidance on developing conceptual model based on theoretical models. (ii) Opportunities blockchain technology can offer to avoid cost and time to check the quality of the returned products at each touch point in reverse logistics. (iii) Role of multiple stakeholder's involvement including governments and the limitation in sharing of information with the existing data capture technologies (e.g. RFID and barcode).

Keywords Reverse logistics · RFID · TAM · Risk-benefit · Blockchain technology · Characteristics

N. Subramanian et al., *Blockchain and Supply Chain Logistics*,
https://doi.org/10.1007/978-3-030-47531-4_8

8.1 Introduction

The digital transformation and the development of e-commerce have created a very sophisticated and highly interconnected world (Kayikci 2018), where logistics sector effectively connects end-to-end supply chain operations (Ceniga and Sukalova 2015). Conventionally, forward logistics effectively ships finished products from the suppliers to the end customers within a precise time window. However, varying returns scheme and mistakes in handling necessitates pool proof mechanisms with technology intervention to seamlessly integrate reverse logistics chain in the closed-loop supply chain. Although automatic identification techniques such as Barcode, Radio Frequency Identification (RFID) etc. have been used in reverse logistics, such technologies do not allow companies to monitor the status of their returns to multiple stakeholders (Rogers and Tibben-Lembke 1999). Hence, the logistics service providers find it difficult to ascertain the quality of returned products. The demand for reverse logistics has risen in recent years with the rise of e-commerce (Prevost 2018), as today's end consumers have a new vision of utilization of purchasing by making eco-conscious decisions (Robinson 2018). The statistics show that the supply chain costs associated with reverse logistics average between 7 and 10% of cost of goods, in addition, the costs of reverse logistics are estimated to be in the range of $750 billion per year (Robinson 2014). Using blockchain technology in reverse logistics has a great potential to alleviate costs, increase efficiency and document responsibility and also improve environmental best practices.

There is a potential to apply blockchain in reverse logistics, since blockchain technology can help information sharing and record every transaction. Also, blockchain is useful to determine the cost of documentation errors, like inaccurate invoicing, late shipping, and returns due to order errors. Similarly, the reverse logistics operations of automotive industry including repairs and maintenance can benefit from blockchain as blockchain can track maintenance records and enhance vehicle performance and longevity (Robinson 2018). Hence, this study tries to explore the use of blockchain technology to address the challenges in reverse logistics. This study tried to explore the application of blockchain technology in reverse logistics regarding tracking of the returned products, and to find out whether and to what extent do the perceived benefits help the users to accept a new technology like blockchain. Specifically, the objective of the study is to answer the following research questions:

- How does blockchain technology benefit reverse logistics process?
- To what extent do the perceived benefits of blockchain allow the logistics professionals to adopt the technology for reverse logistics processes?

The study identifies how blockchain technology can benefit the reverse logistics process and how the perceived benefits may help the users adopt the technology while overcoming the perceived risks using the Technology Acceptance Model (TAM). The results of the study indicate that blockchain technology can enable the all the stakeholders to monitor the status of the products even if it is already sold. Hence, blockchain can benefit the reverse logistics process by simplifying the inspection process and by ensuring the quality of the returned products.

8.2 Motivation

In the past, researchers ignored the reverse flow (from the point of consumption to the point of production) of supply chain (Bernon and Cullen 2007). Besides, logistics industry has also realized that a better understanding of product returns and efficient reverse logistics can be a competitive advantage (Stock and Mulki 2009). Although the concepts of reverse logistics have been well defined and the importance of reverse logistics has been raising, companies implementing reverse logistics are still rare (Ho et al. 2012). Sharma et al. (2011) indicated that one of the challenges in reverse logistics process was the returned products quality. In products return, most of the returned products quality, particularly the time-sensitive products with high marginal value (HMV) for return, are not uniform, like that it could be faulty, damaged, or simply unwanted by the customers. These products return requires the logistics providers to sort, assess the quality and take disposal decision quickly, because the value of these high marginal value products depreciates with time as it moves through the return process to its ultimate disposal decision (Blackburn et al. 2004). Nevertheless, the existing data capturing technologies (i.e. RFID, barcode) only provide the logistics providers the location information of the returned products, but fail to monitor the returned products in various stage of the product life cycle. Therefore, the logistics providers do not know the quality of the returned products and need extra time and money for further quality inspection. Moreover, managers are often unaware of the magnitude of these losses and of how they occur.

In addition, the customers sometimes need to report the materials of the returned products to the logistics providers to ensure that the returned products are qualified to be recycled, however, the customers always do not know the materials and the logistics providers need to take extra time on inspection, which is time-consuming and cost-intensive (Agrawal et al. 2015).

The current reverse logistics data capturing technologies failed to track the returned product information (i.e. materials and quality) in the whole product life cycle (Gu and Liu 2013). And many researchers have carried out researches on tracking reverse logistics products quality for a long time, and quickly expanded to the information on product life cycles to help make better logistics decisions. For example, Thierry et al. (1995) suggested that putting sensors in products to record their information in their product life cycle, but this idea failed due to higher initial costs and lack of technology support. Therefore, an information technology that has the ability to record the products quality information in the whole product life cycle.

Moreover, the development of reverse logistics in Turkey and Hong Kong is low and it is not popular among industries. Only a few industries such as the mobile phone industry (Chan and Chan 2008) and the publishing industry (Wu and Cheng 2006) have adopted it. Ho et al. (2012) concluded that because companies are not familiar with reverse logistics, its awareness in Turkey and Hong Kong is not much importance. In addition, several factors including investment on information technologies, government support will affect the implementation of reverse logistics in Turkey and Hong Kong (Ho et al. 2012).

8.3 Challenges

Gu and Liu (2013) proposed an information system in reverse logistics should have the following characteristics: (i) providing real-time data about the returned products, (ii) keeping accurate and uninterrupted data, (iii) ensuring the quality of the returned products, (iv) preventing data access from the third party, and (v) traceability of past history.

- Providing real-time data about the returned products (Track and Trace): Real-time data helps the reverse logisticians to know the location of products and decide how to deal with reverse logistics products. In addition, real-time data enables intermediaries to track and trace accurately the returned products (Dissanayake 2007).

- Keeping accurate and uninterrupted record of data (Data Accuracy): Many products have a life span of more than ten years, therefore, how to keep an accurate and uninterrupted record of data during such a long period is an issue in reverse logistics information system. In addition, returns are difficult to accurately forecast (Srivastava and Srivastava 2006), if the data is not accurate, it will be a loss for business.
- Ensuring the quality of the returned products (Returned Products Quality): The purpose of reverse logistics is to recycle resources and reuse backflow products, as a result, it is important that the returned products must be in good quality for recycle, reuse or reproduce. If the returned products are not qualified to be recycled, reused, or reproduce d, there will be a loss to reverse logisticians.
- Preventing data access from the third party (Data Security): Data access security is a core part of the entire reverse logistics information system (Mu and Ma 2014), because the logistics companies can prevent competitors accessing sensitive data (i.e. customer identity), and thus may retain an advantage in the marketplace (Pinna and Carrus 2012).
- Traceability of past history: Logistics providers can save time from collecting this data from the end-customers. End-customers sometimes fail to provide this data accurately to the logistics providers.

There is a data security problem with RFID and barcode because they are world-readable, so anyone with a RFID scanner can obtain the sensitive information from the RFID tags. Moreover, RFID is hackable where the information can be altered. Therefore, this section will discuss how does blockchain technology help reverse logistics operations in terms of (i) track and trace of the returned products, (ii) data accuracy, (iii) returned products quality, (iv) data security, and (v) traceability of past history, and finally illustrate the potential benefits that blockchain technology may bring to reverse logistics process.

(i) Track and Trace of the Returned Products: Once the transaction is entered to blockchain, block will create and keep hosting a continuously growing number of records. These records will update instantly and the data cannot be deleted or altered anymore (Casey and Wong 2017) to make sure that no one can alter the data and prevent fraud transactions. The current location of any returned product is available by examining the current state of block. As a result, blockchain helps transfer the real-time data of the returned products (i.e. the location of the products) to the reverse logisticians instantly which helps reverse logisticians have a better expectation of the returned products arrival time. In addition, knowing the location of a returned product (i.e. traceability of material or component) for recovery or remanufactured can help reduce uncertainty in the product (Kouhizadeh and Sarkis 2018).

(ii) Data Accuracy: Every data updated to blockchain must be verified by all of its users, and all data is protected by public key encryption techniques which prevent the sensitive data to be hacked by the irrelevant parties (Aitzhan and Svetinovic 2016). Generally, all data in blockchain need not be authenticated by the auditors to ensure that all data is absolutely true and complete (Baker and Steiner 2015). Further, the timestamping function of the blockchain technology, in conjunction with the audit trail, provides an accurate record of who, what, where and when a product might have been changed over a given period of time (Flynn 2017). In reverse logistics operations, accurate data is important because it helps the reverse logisticians to determine whether the product status is suitable for recycle, reuse, or reproduce. As a result, blockchain technology help reverse logisticians make better decisions.

(iii) Returned Products Quality: Consistent with the literature (i.e. Asif 2011), all respondents agreed that quality uncertainty of the returned products is the barrier in reverse logistics operations, because the suppliers do not have enough information on the returned products due to the lack of transparency. Nevertheless, blockchain technology can be a solution to quality uncertainty. Blockchain technology provides an opportunity to the suppliers to better understand the quality of the products before making recycle decision.

(iv) Data Security: "permissioned" blockchain is suitable for sensitive data (Wild et al. 2015). Permissioned blockchain offers privacy, security, and scalability to the users and the data. In reverse logistics operations, some information is sensitive and should not be seen by the irrelevant parties, therefore, the end customers can set up a permissioned blockchain with their suppliers to ensure that the sensitive data is not visible to or hacked by the irrelevant parties. When blockchain transparency is used to track product throughout its life cycle, stored personal information can not only be protected, but can also be removed without compromise.

(v) Traceability of past history: Information such as production materials and transaction s are related to that products will be recorded on block, which is permanent and unalterable (Baker and Steiner 2015). Each block is then chained to the next block in a chronological order, which is validated and accurate. Therefore, if the logistics providers want to know the past history (i.e. production materials) of the returned products, they can view that information via blockchain instead of asking the end-customers.

8.4 Blockchain Application for Reverse Logistics

The respondents in this study are the experts in Turkey and Hong Kong based logistics and IT companies. The sample selection is based on the following guidelines: (i) the respondents have been working in logistics industry for several years; (ii) the respondents should have a solid experience in reverse logistics, or (iii) the respondents should have academic background on logistics or gained the relevant knowledge through experience. Table 8.1 shows the details of these respondents.

This study was undertaken between June and December of 2018. It involved a broad review of extant literature and ten semi-structured interviews with consenting participants. Interviews were conducted through electronic platform (Skype etc.) and face-to-face, were scheduled to last between 45 minutes to an hour and were recorded for future analysis. All participants interviewed are professionals with reverse logistics experience. Respecting the anonymity of the respondent, no personal information and company name is presented in this study. The conversations were then transcribed and sent back to the participants to ensure that all the data collected were valid and reliable. The transcripts were used for further analysis in this study.

Table 8.1 Respondents profile

Respondent	*Country*	*Position*	*Working year*	*Experience/education level*
1	Hong Kong	Logistics Manager	17 years	A Logistics Degree holder
2	Hong Kong	Assistant Logistics Manager	12 years	A Logistics Degree holder
3	Hong Kong	Logistics Manager	10 years	A Logistics Degree holder
4	Hong Kong	Project Manager	20 years	Working in logistics sector for 20 years
5	Hong Kong	IT Manager	10 years	Have a solid experience in IT
6	Turkey	Logistics Manager	22 years	A Logistics Degree holder
7	Turkey	Logistics Manager	24 years	A Logistics Degree holder
8	Turkey	IT Manager	11 years	Working in logistics sector for 10 years
9	Turkey	Business Development Manager	15 years	Working in logistics consulting sector for 15 years
10	Turkey	Project Manager	15 years	Working in logistics sector for 15 years

Source Author

Retrieval of data is conducted with objectivity and no presumptions or bias from the researcher. In order to improve the validity of the findings, ten semi-structured interviews with the reverse logistics professionals were conducted as well as the secondary data in blockchain technology was studied with the support of several white papers published by leading consulting companies. In terms of internal validity, since previous research on blockchain and reverse logistics are mere and rare, therefore, internal validity is not applicable to this study. However, in terms of external validity, ten semi-structured interviews and secondary data were established and studied to generate broader knowledge of the research topic to enable generalization of potential implications. Finally, draft interview reports were sent to the interviewees for their reviews.

In order to improve the reliability of the findings, ten semi-structured interviews with the professionals were recorded to ensure that the transcription process is error free. Moreover, the transcripts were checked by the authors and the respondents to avoid obvious mistakes. However, since the chosen research field is evolving and new to the academia, therefore, these factors should be taken into account and should be recognized by others to replicate the research.

A qualitative data analysis software, NVivo was used to analyse the ten datasets. The purpose is to check if there is any pattern among their responses. Their responses were coded, analysed, and finally compared with the existing literatures to generate new findings. This study follows the steps proposed by Hilal and Alabri (2013) to analyse the data.

Analysis started with the creation of a new project which named "blockchain technology", and one source folder within the said project. There are ten transcripts in Microsoft Word format for this study. After all transcripts are transferred, the next step is coding, "the process of putting together extracts (across documents) that are related to each other into basins called nodes" (Richards 2005). In particular, all transcripts are thoroughly read and nodes are created in the process to house relevant text from the transcripts.

All respondents indicated that their company are currently using electronic data interchange (EDI) and barcode in reverse logistics operations. They also agreed that such technologies cannot deal with the problem of quality uncertainty of the returned products as they didn't know the products quality in advance and mainly relied on warehouse staff to check and inspect the returned products. They concluded that quality uncertainty is the main barrier in reverse logistics operations according to their experience, which is consistent with the literature (Asif 2011). As stated by one of the respondents:

> Normally, what we received is different from what we are expected to receive.

Regarding the drivers to engage in a new technology (i.e. blockchain technology), most respondents pointed out that ease of use and less training time will be the factors that affect their willingness to adopt blockchain technology. As stated by one of the respondents:

> …because we don't want to put extra time on training our staff to use this new technology, because time is money in our industry.

Besides, all respondents indicated that if blockchain technology can solve quality uncertainty problem, they will consider adopting it. As stated by one of the respondents:

> If the blockchain technology can really solve the reverse logistics barriers, such as the quality uncertainty, our company will consider adopting it.

Regarding the barriers to engage in a new technology, all respondents agreed that they are unfamiliar with this technology due to insufficient government promotion (Ho et al. 2012). Besides, some of them agreed that they will not consider blockchain technology because reverse logistics is not mainstream of operations in their company which is consistent with the literature (Chan and Chan 2008; Ho et al. 2012).

The respondents agreed that quality uncertainty is common in reverse logistics operations. For example, some customers always returned the products which are in low quality or not exactly the products to be returned to them which caused them extra cost and time to inspect the returned products. Besides, they agreed that the existing data capturing technologies (RFID and barcode) failed to track the product status after the products were sold to the end customers. The respondents agreed that blockchain technology can facilitate authentication, ownership and authorization of returns and credits easily real-time while in store, online or at any partner organization enabling positive customer experience, while eliminating return counterfeiting for retailers.

All respondents agreed that blockchain technology might be able to address quality uncertainty as it can ensure traceability. They believed that blockchain technology might benefit the reverse logistics operations by speeding up the reverse logistics process as blockchain can monitor the product status even after they were sold to the end customers. In addition, blockchain with smart contracts, IoT, RFID and other technology solutions might become more powerful to solve the quality problems. Therefore, reverse logistics professionals can know the current status of the products (e.g. quality) and eliminate the extra cost and time on inspecting the quality of the returned products. Moreover, the respondents believed that blockchain technology might help deal with the counterfeit products in reverse logistics because sometimes the customers returned the counterfeit products instead of the authentic products to earn money. When such instances occur, the reverse logistics professionals are unable to distinguish the counterfeit products from the authentic products. Nevertheless, blockchain might prevent this issue because every component or material of the product were recorded on blockchain from the first day of production and the records were either undeletable or unamendable. As a result, the customers cannot return counterfeit products anymore because the original product's materials and components will be recorded on blockchain while the counterfeit products' will not be recorded. The respondents noted that they may take few years to learn and apply blockchain technology in reverse logistics operations. Respondents also mentioned that applying use cases of reverse logistics into blockchain trials might be important point in achieving positive return on investment, so that blockchain can move beyond proof-of-concept and leads to full network deployment.

8.5 Framework with Future Directions

Technology Acceptance Model (TAM) is a robust but parsimonious theory to explain a adoption of particular information system or technology (Olushola and Abiola 2017). Many studies have proposed extended models based on TAM. Many researches added new variables based on the TAM including human behaviour in adoption of a new technology. For example, Li and Huang (2009) applied Theory of Perceived Risk to TAM to examine how does perceived risk affect the user's behavioural intentions towards the adoption of online shopping channel. They found that perceived risk negatively influenced perceived usefulness and perceived ease of use towards the use of online shopping channel, and hence reduced the user's attitude and behavioural intentions towards the adoption of online shopping channel. Li and Huang (2009) explained that because the outcomes associated with the adoption of a new technology were rarely known, which in turn, generated the perceived risk to the users and then reduced their intentions to adopt a new technology.

Nevertheless, Li and Huang (2009) did not consider variable which can capture motivation of users to adopt a new technology despite perceived risk negatively influencing the users' behavioural intentions towards a new technology. Perceived risk includes performance risk of the new technology, because the technology is new to the users and the actual result might not be consistent with theory. Therefore, this

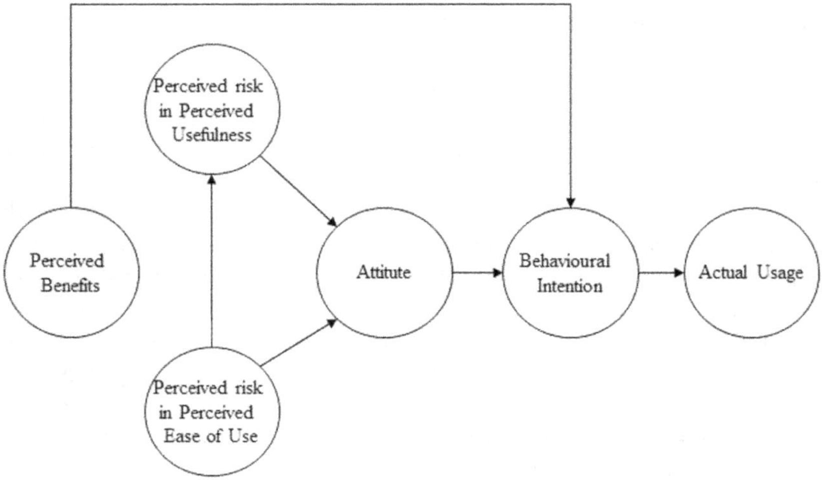

Fig. 8.1 Risk benefit model for blockchain technology applications in reverse logistics (*Source* Author)

study attempted to add a new variable called "perceived benefits" in Li and Huang's (2009) model to further explain how does perceived benefits affect user's behavioural intentions towards blockchain technology. Perceived benefits refer to the benefits that blockchain technology may bring to the complex processes of reverse logistics, such as simplifying the inspection process and helping the logistics provider to understand the returned products in advance to avoid unqualified returns, since blockchain provides an evidentiary trail of information that can be used quickly to return to the point of origin. Figure 8.1 shown demonstrates a modified TAM. The idea to include benefits in the TAM model is from the conventional risk benefit thinking of weighing benefits against using a new technology which is seen as a risk.

8.6 Key Takeaways

Future research can be directed to understand how blockchain technology can impact specific reverse logistics processes. Specifically, numerous studies are essential to overcome potential challenges in adopting blockchain technology in reverse logistics operations. This study found that perceived benefits can offset the negative influence of perceived risk for adopting blockchain. However, it was limited to interviews and without further empirical testing. Hence, future large scale empirical evidence on testing the effect of perceived benefits against perceived risk in adopting a new technology would be needed. Besides, some scholars such as. Amoako-Gyampah, and Salam (2004) found that adequate training helped the users to deal with perceived risk, so future research on addressing those perceived risk for blockchain adoption would also be needed. Future scholars could think about generalising the views from a large sample from both emerging and developed economies. Therefore, their perspective on specific topics such as drivers and barriers of adopting a new technology in reverse logistics would add value for practitioners to engage in reverse logistics operations.

References

Agrawal, S., Singh, R. K., & Murtaza, Q. (2015). A literature review and perspectives in reverse logistics. *Resources, Conservation and Recycling, 97,* 76–92.

Aitzhan, N. Z., & Svetinovic, D. (2016). Security and privacy in decentralized energy trading through multi-signatures, blockchain and anonymous messaging streams. *IEEE Transactions on Dependable and Secure Computing, 15*(5), 840–852.

Amoako-Gyampah, K., & Salam, A. F. (2004). An extension of the technology acceptance model in an ERP implementation environment. *Information & Management, 41,* 731–745.

Asif, R. (2011). Reverse logistics: RFID the key to optimality. *Journal of Industrial Engineering and Management, 4*(2), 281–300.

Baker, J., & Steiner, J. (2015). *Blockchain: The solution for transparency in product*. Available at: https://www.provenance.org/whitepaper. Accessed 28 July 2017.

Bernon, M., & Cullen, J. (2007). An integrated approach to managing reverse logistics. *International Journal of Logistics: Research and Applications, 10*(1), 41–56.

Blackburn, J. D., Guide, D., Souza, G. C., & Wassenhove, L. V. (2004). Reverse supply chains for commercial returns. *California Management Review, 46*(2), 6–22.

Casey, M. J., & Wong, P. (2017). Global supply chain are about to get better, thanks to blockchain. *Harvard Business Review*. Available at: https://hbr.org/2017/03/global-supply-chains-are-about-to-get-better-thanks-to-blockchain. Accessed 21 September 2018.

Ceniga, P., & Sukalova, V. (2015). Future of logistics management in the process of globalization. *Procedia Economics and Finance, 26*, 160–166.

Chan, T. S. F., & Chan, H. K. (2008). A survey on reverse logistics system of mobile phone industry in Hong Kong. *Management Decision, 46*(5), 702–708.

Dissanayake, K. D. (2007). *Reverse Logistics and Information Management Issues in Manufacturing and E-Business Industries* (PhD). RMIT University.

Flynn, C. (2017). *Product life cycle management on a blockchain network*. EY. Available at: http://www.ey.com/Publication/vwLUAssets/ey-product-life-cycle-management-using-blockchain/$FILE/ey-product-life-cycle-management-using-blockchain.pdf. Accessed 10 December 2018.

Gu, Y. X., & Liu, Q. Q. (2013). Research on the application of the internet of things in reverse logistics information management. *Journal of Industrial Engineering and Management, 6*(4), 923–973.

Hilal, A., & Alabri, S. (2013). Using NVivo for data analysis in qualitative research. *International Interdisciplinary Journal of Education, 2*(2), 181–186.

Ho, G. T. S., Choy, K. L., Lam, C. H. Y., & Wong, D. W. C. (2012). Factors influencing implementation of reverse logistics: A survey among Hong Kong businesses. *Measuring Business Excellence, 16*(3), 29–46.

Kayikci, Y. (2018). E-Commerce in logistics and supply chain management. In M. Khosrow-Pour (Ed.), *Encyclopedia of information science and technology* (4th ed., pp. 5367–5377, Chapter 466). Hershey: IGI Global.

Kouhizadeh, M., & Sarkis, J. (2018). Blockchain practices, potentials, and perspectives in greening supply chains. *Sustainability, 10*, 3652.

Li, Y. H., & Huang, J. W. (2009). Applying theory of perceived risk and technology acceptance model in the online shopping channel. *World Academy of Science, Engineering and Technology, 53*, 919–925.

Mu, R. H., & Ma, Y. L. (2014). The design and implementation of reverse logistics management information system. *Journal of Chemical and Pharmaceutical Research, 6*(5), 2024–2027.

Olushola, T., & Abiola, J. O. (2017). The efficacy of technology acceptance model: A review of applicable theoretical models in information technology researches. *Journal of Research in Business and Management, 4*(11), 70–83.

Pinna, R., & Carrus, P. (2012). Reverse logistics and the role of fourth party logistics provider. In A. Groznik & Y. Xiong (Eds.), *Pathways to Supply Chain Excellence* (1st ed., Chapter 6). Croatia: InTech.

Prevost, C. (2018). *Fr8 Network: Blockchain's powerful potential for reverse logistics*. Available at: https://www.freightwaves.com/news/blockchain/fr8-network-reverse-logistics. Accessed 1 September 2018.

Richards, L. (2005). *Handling qualitative data: A practical guide* (3rd ed.). London: Sage.

Robinson, A. (2014). *Top 3 benefits of a reverse logistics management program*. Available at: https://cerasis.com/2014/02/27/reverse-logistics-management/. Accessed 21 September 2018.

Robinson, A. (2018). *Use of blockchain in supply chain & logistics: Looking to examples across industries for better understanding*. Available at: https://cerasis.com/2018/07/30/use-of-blockchain-in-supply-chain-logistics/. Accessed 1 September 2018.

Rogers, D. S., & Tibben-Lembke, R. S. (1999). *Going Backwards: Reverse Logistics Trends and Practices*. Reverse Logistics Executive Council.

Sharma, S. K., Panda, B. N., Mahapatra, S. S., & Sahu, S. (2011). Analysis of barriers for reverse logistics: An Indian perspective. *International Journal of Modeling and Optimization, 1*(2), 101–106.

Srivastava, S. K., & Srivastava, R. K. (2006). Managing product returns for reverse logistics. *International Journal of Physical Distribution & Logistics Management, 36*(7), 524–546.

Stock, J. R., & Mulki, J. P. (2009). Product returns processing: An examination of practices of manufacturers, wholesalers/distributors, and retailers. *Journal of Business Logistics, 30*(1), 33–62.

Thierry, M., Salomon, M., Van Nunen, J., & Van Wassenhove, L. (1995). Strategic issues in product recovery management. *California Management Review, 37*(2), 114–135.

Wild, J., Arnold, M., & Stafford, P. (2015). *Technology: Banks seek the key to blockchain*. Financial Times, 1 November. Available at: https://www.ft.com/content/eb1f8256-7b4b-11e5-a1fe-567b37f80b64. Accessed 23 April 2017.

Wu, Y. C. J., & Cheng, W. P. (2006). Reverse logistics in the publishing industry: China, Hong Kong and Taiwan. *International Journal of Physical Distribution & Logistics Management, 36*(7), 507–523.

Index

N. Subramanian et al., *Blockchain and Supply Chain Logistics*,
https://doi.org/10.1007/978-3-030-47531-4

U

V

CPSIA information can be obtained
at www.ICGtesting.com
Printed in the USA
LVHW081629210620
658633LV00020B/1285